'*Shareplicity* is the perfect Just in Time book!

Given the global economic turbulence, the current public health crisis and the entry to our market of so many inexperienced day traders, Danielle's book is the perfect brainfood that alerts us to both the opportunities and the risks in our current share market. With the importance of equities to both our economy and our own wealth management and superannuation funds, this book is essential reading, and rereading! The author has drawn on her extensive global and local experience and her lucid flowing style to ensure that this book not only offers fresh and powerful insights, but is also reader-friendly for us all.

I commend this book as essential reading for all those who seek robust and valuable insights into the share investing. Its currency and wisdom make it a unique resource in a market too often overloaded with shallow or outdated advice.'

Dr Roger Collins, Emeritus Professor at the University of NSW

'A clean and crisp introduction to our share market, which manages to capture both traditional principles of analysis along with the key themes in front of Australian investors today. Ecuyer is as good on BHP as she is on CSL and as up to date on Wesfarmers as on the "buy now pay later" brigade: a well written and attractively structured guidebook on shares for the Australian investor.'

James Kirby, Wealth Editor, *The Australian*

'At a time when the investment world seems to be suffering from information overload, Danielle Ecuyer has sorted out what is important and necessary and has put it in this book. It covers all aspects of investing in the stock market, from how to buy a share to how to construct your own winning portfolio. In particular, as a former stock market analyst, and now a full-time investor, she is able to present very useful guidance on selecting shares with long-term profit potential. This excellent book is highly recommended for both new and experienced investors.'

Martin Roth, author of the bestselling annual publication *Top Stocks*

'When very new investors approach me for guidance, I have tended to send them to a smattering of online resources. This in itself is a challenge as the pieces of the puzzle can be disjointed. Not anymore. *Shareplicity* is now the single resource to get every new and curious investor immediately on target. It provides an effective roadmap to not only understand broad share market concepts, but also provides a foundation to build a sensible portfolio. I know five people who need *Shareplicity* right now.'

Nick Radge, Head of Trading and Research, thechartist.com.au

'With its easy-to-read format, *Shareplicity* takes its readers through the basics, ensuring they understand how the market actually works, giving helpful summaries at the end of each chapter. It then guides them through the steps required to develop a fundamentally sound portfolio, acknowledging that it is not only the numbers that drive the markets, but equally important, market sentiment. Based on Danielle's years of practical experience, this well written book will appeal to both new and experienced investors of all ages.'

Janene Murdoch, Owner and Manager, specialist investment bookstore Educatedinvestor.com.au

Shareplicity

A simple approach to share investing

DANIELLE ECUYER

Author note

Just as this book was going to press in March 2020, the world entered a period of lockdown to stop the spread of COVID-19. The Australian share market crashed from its mid-February peak and fell some 37 per cent at a speed and ferocity not seen since the October 1987 crash. Launching a book on share investing seemed fanciful at that time, so we 'stopped the presses'.

Six weeks on, the world is still turning, and we are all trying to establish some modicum of normality. Share markets have responded with vigour and enthusiasm to the global efforts by Central Banks to shore up our financial systems and concerted global efforts to develop effective treatments and a vaccine for the coronavirus. At the end of April, the Australian market is up some 18 per cent from the March 23rd lows.

There's no denying these are unprecedented times for share investors. However, the themes discussed in *Shareplicity* still hold true and have proudly passed the COVID-19 test. Sure, in most cases, share prices are considerably lower now than when I finished the final numerical edits on February 14th, 2020; meaning for new or existing investors this is an excellent time to brush up on share market basics, do some research into how to buy shares and construct a share portfolio to grow your wealth for the future.

As you'll hear me say a few times throughout the book, good quality shares with strong balance sheets and cash flow will stand the test of time and see their way through the 2020 recession. Please bear in mind company earnings and dividend forecasts and share price targets shown in *Shareplicity* are pre the coronavirus health shock and the recession Australia and the world are now experiencing. They will have been adjusted and continue to be so. What is more important than the forecasts, as they are predictions and subject to change regularly, are the themes of the book.

If I were to pick the three companies discussed in *Shareplicity* that have hit more of a speed hump than most, they would be Sydney Airport, Transurban and Macquarie. But all three were, and will remain, resilient companies with good access to capital if needed. As quality businesses, they will manage high risk and extreme uncertainty and find pathways for future growth.

If COVID-19 has taught me one thing, it is not to become complacent when share investing. Even in the bad times, with the huge liquidity drawdowns of March 2020, the first shares to bounce were the bulk of those highlighted in *Shareplicity*.

First published in 2020 by Major Street Publishing Pty Ltd
E | info@majorstreet.com.au W | majorstreet.com.au M | +61 421 707 983

A catalogue record for this book is available from the National Library of Australia

NATIONAL LIBRARY OF AUSTRALIA

ISBN: 978-0-6486626-9-3

Cover design by Peter Reardon
Author photograph taken by Joshua Morris
Internal design by Production Works
Printed in Australia by McPhersons's Printing

10 9 8 7 6 5 4

Contents

Contents

Ford v Ferrari:
what makes or breaks a company

What does the Hollywood movie *Ford v Ferrari* have to do with share investing? Everything and nothing!

It's 1966, and the scene is the world's oldest and most prestigious endurance racing car event, the 24-hour Le Mans, in France. British racing car driver Ken Miles is leading in the final lap to secure the first ever victory for America's Ford Motor Company.

What happens next shocks a nation and the world's racing community. Even though Ken Miles is in line for the world's triple crown for endurance races that year, Ford's head of public relations tells Miles to slow down and allow the second- and third-placed Ford cars to cross the line with him.

This secures a triple-place win for the Ford Motor Company. It's a global photo opportunity for the media hungry company and a triple slapdown to Enzo Ferrari, whose two Ferraris withdrew at the halfway mark of the race.

Ironically, the photo finish cost Ken Miles the win, as another Ford car driven by New Zealander Bruce McLaren, who finished third, won on a technicality. Le Mans is renowned for its unusual start: drivers stand opposite their cars and sprint to their vehicles at the line-up. The winner is measured not on time but on distance travelled over the 24 hours. McLaren's car had been 8 metres behind Miles's so, in slowing down to allow for the other cars, Miles lost the winner's trophy by a margin of 8 metres. It was a cruel outcome for Miles for what amounted to a marketing stunt.

Company culture: behind the scenes

This action said so much about the culture and ethos of the Ford Motor Company and what mattered to it. There was certainly no room for individual stars; the triple-place win was for the greater good of the company and because the CEO wanted to bask in his victory over his Italian nemesis.

For the first time in history, Henry Ford II, grandson and name sake of one of the most famous men in manufacturing history, claimed supremacy in the world of endurance car racing. This was a win like no other. This was a personal battle of the egos between the European king of prestige cars, Enzo Ferrari, and his enemy in spirit from the other side of the Atlantic, Henry Ford II.

Three years earlier, in an attempt to revive the flagging image and sales of the Ford Motor Company amid increased competition and pressures from General Motors, Ford II made a failed attempt to buy the illustrious but bankrupt Ferrari group. A strategic takeover would have bolstered the Ford image, transferred the Ford name and brand across the pond and given them a higher profile in the prestigious world of car racing.

The attempt not only battered the ego of Ford's CEO, with Enzo Ferrari accepting a higher offer from Gianni Agnelli's Fiat group, it also ignited a burning desire to take on Enzo at his own game and beat him on the racetrack at Le Mans, the toughest endurance car race in the world.

Ferrari, the most successful motor racing company, was about quality, small scale and premium pricing. Ford, in contrast, was a car of the masses, being squeezed by competitors. Henry Ford II wanted what he didn't have: prestige, racing power and respect on the world stage. His dream, as history shows, came true and the Ford GT40 went on to win a total of four successive Le Mans races.

To achieve Ford II's goal, the Ford Motor Company looked outside of its traditional management structure and enlisted the help of former Le Mans winner Carroll Shelby, played by Matt Damon in the movie *Ford v Ferrari*. He, in turn, recruited his friend Ken Miles, brilliantly brought to life by actor Christian Bale.

Against the odds, these two men rebuilt Ford's failing GT40 racing car prototype using unconventional methods and all the mechanical engineering skills the team could muster. The journey was not without conflict and disagreement, however. Ford's management style and the behaviour of his minions was at odds with the entrepreneurial and maverick style of the two racing car drivers. In one scene in the movie, a folder summarising the progress of the GT40 Ford car passed through as many as four different pairs of hands in a single room before it was finally passed to the big man himself, Henry Ford II. This was clearly a cumbersome and heavy management structure.

The company set up internal teams to compete against each other for the Le Mans victory. Shelby and Miles were trying to snatch the five-year winning streak from the victorious Ferrari.

The 24-hour race is brutal – travelling at speeds up to 218 miles per hour in those conditions in 1966 stretched both human and car to the limit.

In the movie, Matt Damon's character, Shelby, explains to Mr Ford that a winning racing car cannot be achieved through paper pushing; it's achieved through track testing and retesting for hours on end by a racing car genius, like Miles.

Ford v Ferrari defines what makes or breaks a company. As the true story unfolds, the scenes illustrate the differences between the politics of the big corporate suits and the brave, hardworking maverick racing car driver 'Happy' Ken Miles, who lost due to politics in the end. The movie shows the manufacturing flaws of Ford's cars versus the tender loving care of the construction of a Ferrari. It depicts the culture wars between the old and new worlds of Italy and the brash, fast-producing ideology of the USA. Most importantly, it shows how ego and culture define a company.

Take a look at *Ford v Ferrari* if you haven't seen it; it offers a window into the many aspects of what drives a company behind the scenes. Corporate culture stems from the top and much of what makes a company tick comes from the chief executive or founder. I talk more about company culture in Chapter 7 and the appendix.

Shares are not just about the numbers

Companies are often defined by investors as a set of numbers or a narrative (a story), and the share or stock (same thing) that investors buy is too often melted down to just a price.

A share is literally a percentage an investor owns of a company, so it's more than just the price or number it trades for on a stock exchange. A company, as the film portrays, is about people, culture, ego, fame and creating fortunes. Some companies are considerably better than others at creating fortunes for their management, employees and shareholders. Some companies have great cultures and offer excellent work environments. Some are noble stewards in their community as well as wealth creators. Companies are so much more than just a price as defined by a share. Not all companies are the same, even if the numbers and ratios that compare them are similar.

If you're a new investor or seeking to become a better investor, you're like the characters of Shelby and Miles. You have a task at hand to create wealth, but you're starting as an underdog. You're not sure what works, or if the advice you're receiving is failing you. You might even be subjected to criticism and suffer self-doubt.

Thankfully your road to success doesn't require driving on and off for 24 hours in extreme conditions at high speed! Like the racing drivers, however, you want to survive the drive and finish with a victory. Even if you can't secure victory, you want to ensure that the trip isn't too painful and that you learn from the experience.

Why perception matters

Not all people see a movie the same way. I was surprised to hear a film critic discussing what sounded like a completely different movie to *Ford v Ferrari*. How could his reality be so far removed from mine? To him, the movie's premise of Ford as the underdog seemed ridiculous. It was a Hollywood fairy tale that showed the might of America winning against the odds. How could a giant of an American company possibly be inferior to a small operator like Ferrari?

However, history tells us that Ford *was* the underdog and Ferrari was the king of racing cars. Ferrari's prestigious and beautifully handmade vehicles were and still are collectors' pieces. The movie was not a fantasy. Nonetheless, everyone has their own opinions and when it comes to share investing, perception matters.

Perception matters because you need to make decisions based on facts and research, not your preconceived ideas about companies and shares. Investors need to examine their own perceptions and learn to challenge them so that they make good financial decisions based on data not emotions. The trick lies in realising your own personal foibles and working around bias to obtain a real and truthful understanding of a narrative and, in turn, a company or market. I show you how to stick with the facts and keep a lid on greed and fear in Chapter 6.

Taking the *Shareplicity* journey

Like the story of *Ford v Ferrari*, share investing is a journey. The best way to approach this journey is to make it fun, achievable and sustainable so you can reach the goals you set. *Shareplicity* is the book you need to guide you on your trip! It takes a logical approach that will help you to learn about and appreciate the factors and issues that matter most.

Shareplicity simplifies the complex with easy-to-understand examples and helpful analogies, and challenges the views held by existing share investors.

Starting with the basics, I take you through the important aspects of shares and how to take control of your investments to create wealth and income, including how to avoid the loss makers and build a portfolio to meet your needs (see Chapters 4, 5, 6 and 9).

Too often the jargon around shares makes them seem complicated, so to get you over this hurdle I explain the language and terminology in Chapter 2, and have also included a glossary at the end of the book. I also show you how to spot the traps of share investing and how to invest at any life stage. You're never too young or too old to learn how to be a better investor and develop real strategies to create wealth, while managing the risks so you can sleep at night.

At my son's school football games I often chuckled to myself as parents, usually dads, chatted excitedly about the latest hot investment tips from their mate – a gold explorer, a biotech start-up that was going to cure cancer or the next big fintech (financial technology company) like Afterpay or Zip. For many, share investing tips come from a friend, a broker or another 'expert'. The hundreds of columns of ink devoted to business, investing, shares and markets can be overwhelming. I call it 'fast news'. Everything is fast now; technology and the internet have opened a Pandora's box of information overload and confusion. Yet information doesn't equal teaching, understanding, good execution, experience and embedding robust investment processes.

In *Shareplicity*, I show you what you need to look for in a company. Finding the right information is a process not of looking for a needle in a haystack but more like viewing a piece of art from a distance. Perspective and clarity can often be better achieved when you don't look for the minutiae. Monet's *Water Lily* masterpieces are at their best from a distance. The colour and movement amass to create the special forms as we step further back from the canvas; the big picture. In Chapter 3 I explain ways to understand the big picture.

When Ford won the Le Mans it was 1966 – it was a time of extraordinary change. We too are living in an era of great change and new risks for investors, with disruption coming from technology, populism, global pandemics and climate change. Chapter 6 aims to make you aware of 21st century trends in share investing so you can make educated decisions.

Chapter 8 gives you all you need to know on indirect investing, including new products like exchange traded funds (ETFs) and how to manage costs and fees when you invest with a managed fund.

Sharing my experience

In the following chapters I bring together my four decades of investment experience, a successful career as an institutional stockbroker advising some of the world's largest fund management clients, and my own experience of making a living from shares.

During my career, I transitioned from being a professional stockbroker to managing share investments, which meant I was now looking after *my* savings, not sprouting ideas for large fund managers. Any skills I mastered during my investment career had to be reworked, expanded on and adjusted. Professional fund managers have predetermined mandates, like beating a specific index or percentage amount each year, but private investing is about keeping and growing your savings to meet short- or long-term financial needs. The two are like chalk and cheese. My journey in share investing has been a path of ongoing learning.

Whether you invest directly (buy and sell your own shares) or indirectly (through passive or managed funds), just like the Ford Motor Company in the story of *Ford v Ferrari* you want to aspire to victory and construct the right vehicle so you can go the distance, which is as important as arriving at the finish line.

Shareplicity's simple approach to share investing will give you the ability to unravel the narratives around companies and shares, and improve your knowledge and performance as you cruise down your own share investment road.

2

Sharepedia:
share investing basics

Investing in shares can be as easy as setting up a bank account, and considerably less onerous, expensive and overwhelming than buying an investment property. The internet has enabled the development of low-cost, easy-to-access online share-trading platforms. Compared to years gone by when share investing was predominantly for the wealthy, online platforms have created a world of opportunity for making money, generating an income and offsetting the ever-dwindling returns on cash deposits in the banks.

However, whether it's constructing a flat pack, creating a new culinary dish or learning a new skill, you need basic knowledge and instructions. Share investing is no different. You need to learn the lingo before you move on to how to choose shares, create a portfolio and make some money.

If you're a newbie investor or you just want to brush up on the basics, the following 'sharepedia' will help you on your way.

Note: Share investing terms, jargon and acronyms used throughout this book are explained in the glossary at the end of the book.

Shares, stocks and exchanges

A share or stock (same thing) is a unit of ownership of a company, property trust or investment trust. Shares are traded on a stock exchange, like the ASX (Australian Securities Exchange), the LSE (London Stock Exchange) or NYSE (New York Stock Exchange). Most countries have a stock exchange, although their levels of regulation, transparency and liquidity differ. Shares are also known as 'investment securities', a broad, generic term given to traded financial assets (shares, bonds and options, for example).

Amsterdam had the first acknowledged stock exchange. It was created in the early 17th century to accommodate the Dutch East India Company (VOC). Shares were issued in the VOC to support business growth (by raising money) and the trading of spices and other commodities from Indonesia and other parts of Asia to Holland. Nowadays, a stock exchange is an electronic platform that allows a buyer and seller from anywhere in the world to transact the share trades.

Countries are classified as either developed markets (like Australia, the USA, the UK and Europe) or emerging markets (like Indonesia, Malaysia and Chile). Depending on the country and the stock exchange, there are different levels of risk and transparency attached to investing in the market. Emerging markets have traditionally been higher risk for many reasons.

Developed markets have the benefit of good liquidity levels (that is, it's easier to trade the shares), good levels of regulation to stop malfeasance, high levels of transparency, and stringent reporting of a company's profits and results. These elements all benefit shareholders and investors.

A collection of shares is called a share portfolio. It's preferable to own a selection of shares in different companies rather than just one share. This is called diversifying and it refers to spreading the risk of share investments; think of the expression 'not putting all your eggs in one basket'.

Types of share investing

Companies can have major shareholders – this could be the owner, the founder or large institutions such as superannuation funds, investment trusts, unit trusts and ETFs. The different avenues for share investment will be explained in considerable detail in the following chapters, but to set the stage, the two broad categories are:

1. direct investing (Chapters 4 to 7)
2. indirect investing, which includes active investment funds and passive investment funds or ETFs (Chapter 8).

Direct investing is when you take the initiative and buy and sell shares on your own behalf, with or without a stockbroker. Indirect investing is when you outsource your money to fund managers – people who invest in a group of shares according to different targets and aims, and in differing structures. Indirect investing is divided into active and passive investment vehicles. In active investment funds, a fund manager personally selects the shares on behalf of the fund. These vehicles come in many different shapes and sizes. Here are some examples:

- **A listed investment trust** (LIT) is a closed fund. This means that a specific amount of money is raised and then invested according to the fund's investment mandate. As LITs are trusts, they have a fixed number of units (shares) that you can buy and sell on the stock exchange – the number of units doesn't change when someone buys or sells. The price of the units can trade around the net tangible asset value (NTA) of the shares: meaning, how much the unit is worth will vary depending upon the underlying value of the shares in the trust.

- **A listed investment company** (LIC) has shares (not units) listed on the stock exchange. Like a LIT, the shares can trade at a discount or premium to the NTA, depending on shareholder demand. The difference between a LIT and LIC is essentially the tax treatment of the structure.

- **A unit trust** is what's termed an open ended share-investment vehicle. This means that, unlike in a listed investment trust, the number of units issued will vary depending upon the demand for them. These types of funds are also actively managed.

- **A self-managed account** (SMA) is a specific account invested in shares, bonds and securities, managed by a fund manager but owned in your name and structured for your needs.

- **A passive investment fund** or ETF is called passive because the fund manager purchases a group of shares that, for example, mirror a share index like the ASX 200 or a sector theme like technology. The fund manager doesn't select which shares to include, but simply matches the index or sector. More recently, however, some fund managers have started active ETFs that are designed to be a low-cost product. These have all the benefits of a passive ETF but the fund manager has some discretion to vary the ETF's holdings.

As the types of funds can seem a bit complex, I'll discuss what they mean for you as an investor in a lot more detail in Chapter 8 and how you can make choices about what works for you.

Individuals are referred to as retail investors; those with more money are referred to as wholesale or sophisticated investors. Most of us are retail investors and as such we're termed 'minority shareholders'. In an ideal world, all shareholders would be treated equally.

Share prices and dividends

Shares are referred to as 'financial assets' because an investor is buying a share of a real company, which has an asset value. As mentioned, shares are a type of instrument created hundreds of years ago for companies to use to raise money, known as equity or shareholders' funds.

When you buy a share, it's called a bid. When you sell a share it's called an offer. In a share market, buyers and sellers input the bid price and offer price on their online share-trading platform, and the prices are matched. More sellers means more offers, and usually this puts downward pressure on the share price. More buyers equals more bids, and the share price goes up. It's simple supply and demand.

This is the same as a property auction; the difference is that rather than people standing around with a paddle or yelling out a bid, the prices and the amounts to buy and sell shares are inputted electronically and shown on a screen.

Shareholders benefit when the share price goes up, because the value of their shareholding has increased. They also benefit from income a share generates via a dividend payment. How many shares you buy will depend on the amount of money you have to invest, the price of each share and how many different types of shares you buy.

Dividends are a very important aspect of share investing – so much so that I've devoted an entire chapter to the topic (Chapter 7). A dividend is the amount per share you are paid in cash, normally twice a year, when you buy and hold a share. Dividends are usually generated from the company's earnings and represent the reward for taking the risk of investing in the company (share).

Dividends and the amount paid per share will vary across the companies you invest in. The most important thing to note is that companies do not have to pay a dividend. It's at the discretion of the company's board, and whether a dividend is paid and how much it is can change depending on the financial health of the company. Not all companies pay dividends.

Australian dividends are unique, due to a tax treatment that was introduced by the Hawke/Keating government in 1987: dividend imputation or franking credits. This change was implemented to avoid double taxation of the income generated by a company and paid to shareholders. Dividends can have a franking credit attached to them, reflecting the tax already paid by the company. This means investors can receive a tax rebate from the Australian Taxation Office (ATO) depending on the proportion of the dividend that is franked. If the dividends are 'fully franked' this means the company has paid a full rate of tax on them already. Note that companies that generate the bulk of their earnings overseas will not be able to pass on the franking credit, as they do not pay tax in Australia.

If you have any queries about franking credits, it's best to check the company's dividend statements and seek professional advice, as the franking credit rebates will change depending upon your own tax status.

I appreciate that this probably seems very abstract and confusing! Chapter 7 will provide an example to make the concept easier to understand.

Dividends, as I've mentioned, are usually paid twice a year in Australia, and companies generally announce the payment with their half-year and full-year profit results. Once the dividend for a share is announced, there is a period in which the share trades cum dividend (Latin for 'with dividend'), until the 'record date' – the last day a shareholder is eligible for the dividend. The day before the record date is called the ex-dividend date. Once a share goes ex-dividend, shareholders are not entitled to another dividend until the next company profit report, six months later. Shares often trade lower on the ex-dividend day to reflect the payment of the dividend, but don't worry – in most cases the share prices recover if the shares are in demand, sometimes in a day or two. The industry term for that is 'carried the dividend'.

I've introduced you to a lot of new terms in this section. Don't worry if it seems like a whole new language – just flick to the glossary at the end of this book for a quick reference guide to shares jargon.

Understanding share indices

In Australia, shares are grouped into two main indices: the S&P/ASX 200 index (ASX 200) and the All Ordinaries index (referred to as the All Ords). All stock exchanges around the world have specific indices, such as the FTSE in the UK and the Dow, S&P 500 and Nasdaq in the USA.

The ASX 200 comprises the top 200 largest companies with listed shares, based on the weightings by market capitalisation. The 'market cap', as it's referred to, is the number of shares on issue times the share price. The index is adjusted quarterly to ensure the top 200 companies are included. As share prices rise and fall, companies can move in and out of the index, because the market capitalisation changes with the price movement.

The shares are identified by stock codes and a corresponding country code. The largest listed companies in Australia are normally fairly consistent. Table 2.1 lists the shares that are generally among the top 20 largest by market cap; for more information on indices, visit the ASX website asx.com.au or the S&P website us.spindices.com.

TABLE 2.1: Australian shares which are often in the top 20 by market capitalisation

Code	Company	Sector
AMC	Amcor	Materials
ANZ	ANZ Banking Group	Financials
BHP	BHP Group	Materials
BXB	Brambles	Industrials
CBA	Commonwealth Bank	Financials
CSL	CSL	Health Care
GMG	Goodman Group	Real Estate
IAG	Insurance Australia	Financials
MQG	Macquarie Group	Financials
NAB	National Australia Bank	Financials
RIO	Rio Tinto	Materials
SCG	Scentre Group	Real Estate
S32	South32	Materials
SUN	Suncorp Group	Financials
TLS	Telstra Corporation	Telecommunications
TCL	Transurban Group	Industrials
WES	Wesfarmers	Consumer Discretionary
WBC	Westpac Banking	Financials
WPL	Woodside Petroleum	Energy
WOW	Woolworths Group	Consumer Staples

The All Ordinaries represents the top 500 listed companies on the ASX and is adjusted annually.

Over time, the performance of the indices is measured and this directly correlates to the underlying movement in share prices. So, when people refer to how much the Aussie share market has gone up, strictly speaking they should refer to which index and the corresponding percentage change.

Dividend returns are not included in the indices. In Australia, dividends can add as much as 4–5 per cent to the annual return of the ASX 200, as some of the largest companies have historically paid out a high dividend relative to the share price (there's more on which companies pay the highest dividends later in the book in Chapter 7).

Investors need to be aware of indices because professional share investment managers often benchmark the performance of their funds against specific indices.

Some investment platforms (such as ETFs) specifically offer a share product that tracks the performance of an index. I discuss these in more depth in Chapter 8.

Within the market, shares are identified according to different groupings. The ASX uses a global industry standard to categorise companies into different sectors. Eleven sectors are classified on the ASX:

1. Communication Services
2. Consumer Discretionary
3. Consumer Staples
4. Energy
5. Financials
6. Health Care
7. Industrials
8. Information Technology
9. Materials
10. Real Estate
11. Utilities.

Professional investors and advisers often create model share portfolios based on the sector weighting in the ASX. The largest sectors in the ASX 200 are Financials, including the banks and insurance companies, at around 30 per cent of the index, followed by Materials at around 20 per cent, which represents the iron producers (BHP and Rio). Health Care is the third-largest sector at over 10 per cent. The weightings then descend to Utilities (AGL), which comprises less than 2 per cent of the index. For most retail investors, it's not necessary to follow the sector weightings, but if you are interested, more information is available at asx.com.au and us.spindices.com.

Good reasons to invest in shares

People buy shares to make money. This happens in two ways:

1. The share price goes up – this is called 'capital appreciation'. Profits are realised once the shares are sold.

2. The company pays its shareholders a dividend or 'distribution' – an income.

It's no different to property investing. When a property investor buys a property, the property value will go up over time (well, that's the plan!) and they also receive rent (an income) from the tenants they lease the property to.

Share investors aim to build a portfolio of shares that grow in value over a period of time at a rate that exceeds cash in the bank and bonds, as shown in Table 2.2. The table also shows that US shares and listed property (i.e. property trusts) outperformed Australian shares over a one-year period. In Chapter 9, I outline how you can obtain exposure to international and US share markets to diversify your investments.

TABLE 2.2: Comparison of returns from Australian shares, bonds and cash as at 30 June 2019

	1 year (% p.a.)	5 years (% p.a.)	10 years (% p.a.)	20 years (% p.a.)	30 years (% p.a.)
Australian shares	11.0	9.0	10.0	8.7	9.4
International shares	11.9	13.2	12.4	4.4	7.2
US shares	16.3	17.5	16.3	5.6	10.3
Australian bonds	9.6	5.1	6.0	6.1	8.2
Listed property	19.3	13.6	14.0	8.0	9.2
Cash	2.0	2.1	3.0	4.3	5.6
Consumer Price Index (CPI)	1.3	1.6	2.1	2.6	2.6

You can use shares as a savings tool at any age. Shares are far more affordable than property; you don't need to go into debt like you do when you take out a mortgage. You don't have to deal with tenants or vacancy periods and there are no management or maintenance fees to pay. Buying an investment property is a far more expensive and capital-intensive exercise than owning shares.

Note: Shares can be bought using debt – known as 'margin lending'. However, this is a high risk proposition and only for experienced investors.

Currently in Australia interest rates are at historic lows, and most experts think this won't change for quite some time. This means that popping cash in the bank to grow your savings isn't going to make you rich!

Companies aim to grow their earnings (net profits) each year. As a unit holder or shareholder, you benefit from the growth in earnings. Most companies pay a dividend, which is a percentage of the profit earned per share, to its shareholders. As mentioned previously, this payment represents reward for the risk you take by holding the shares. Depending on the share, the dividend yield can reach 4 per cent p.a.

Shares can deliver what's referred to as a total return. A total return equals the capital gain as a percentage over a 12-month period plus the dividend yield.

Historically, shares (excluding dividends) have delivered an average 10 per cent p.a. compound return over time. In a low-interest-rate world, the total return of shares is expected to decline. However, even an average return of 5 to 7 per cent would still provide investors with better capital growth than putting the money in the bank.

How to buy and sell shares

Shares are traded electronically on the Australian Securities Exchange (ASX) and on share markets around the world (like the USA, Europe and Asia). The internet allows Australians to invest anywhere in the world. Share markets trade for around six to seven hours a day, five days of the week, normally. They're closed for holidays.

There are two ways you can invest in shares in Australia:

1. You can buy and sell shares through companies or online platforms that charge an investor a fee to conduct the transaction. The fee is normally expressed as a percentage of the value of the trade, but, luckily for you, low-cost share-trading platforms have reduced the cost per trade to as low as $9.50.

2. Traditional private client stockbrokers can make your share transactions for you; they will also provide share investment advice and research on the companies. As they're adding value by offering these services, the costs of investing through them are higher.

Low-cost platforms offer a less personalised service and less company research, but the low cost of transacting is appealing, especially for smaller investors. It's a no-frills option.

Once you've set up a share-trading account, you can buy your first share (I show you how to select shares from Chapter 4 onwards). You can invest as little as $500, depending on the share-trading platform you choose to use. Smaller amounts may be bought after a shareholding is created. You can invest your savings in shares at regular intervals, to drip-feed your capital into the share market.

Have a look at the example from my share-trading platform in Figure 2.1. It shows an order to BUY 200 Telstra shares at a price of $3.60. Most share-trading platforms will also give you the market depth figures, showing how many shares are being bid for, how many are on offer and at what price.

FIGURE 2.1: Screenshot of a Telstra share purchase transaction

A market order means the order is filled by the computer, usually at the offer price.

You can see the brokerage and cost (shown in the bottom of the screen) is $10 in this example.

Investors can set a price limit (in this example it's $3.60) and only buy the shares if there's a seller willing to sell at this price. Or they can buy 'at market', which means they're matched with the next buyer at the price on offer at the time.

They can leave their bid open for one day (after which it expires) if it's not immediately matched with a seller. Or they can leave their offer open for a set period of time, with an expiry date showing.

Once you buy your shares, you're identified by either an SRN (shareholder reference number) or a HIN (holder identification number). The SRN means it's issuer sponsored: every time you buy a share you'll receive a different SRN from the issuer and you'll be identified by a 10- or 11-digit number preceded by an I.

If you buy your shares through a stockbroker or an online platform the shares will be CHESS sponsored and you'll have a HIN, which is a unique 10-digit number preceded by an X. All the shares you buy through a stockbroker or online platform will identify you with a HIN.

CHESS is the ASX developed and owned clearing house for shares; it's the technology that allows the change of ownership from buyer to seller and vice versa.

Shareholdings are documented and held by share registries such as Link Market Services and Computershare, and accounts can be accessed online.

The current settlement period for Australian shares is T plus 2, meaning the trade date plus two days. Most share-trading platforms link to a bank account for the withdrawal of funds for purchases and the deposit of funds after sales and dividends.

Costs are important and should be kept to a minimum, as the cost of transactions erodes the return on the share investment.

Trading, charting and shorting

You may have heard of share traders (and day traders in the dotcom boom) making squillions of dollars from the share market.

It's true, some people like to trade shares, which means they only own them for a very short period of time. These 'traders' aim to identify any share that has been sold down (which they therefore think is 'cheap') and is expected to experience a price increase in the short term. Traders use tools such as charts and follow trends like momentum. This refers to when a share is either moving very strongly upwards or downwards. I talk more about charting in Chapter 9 when I discuss the Dow theory.

Charting looks at the share price charts and creates a theory about how to predict future price movements. Traders use what are called stop-losses: if a share falls by a certain percentage, say 25 per cent, they just sell. Traders jump on and off shares, so to speak, and look for a quick turn. Trading requires a certain commitment to watching and acting on share price movements or using specifically designed computer models, known as algorithms. Traders can make good money, but they can also lose money. Many have specific models they employ and volatility is their friend; a stock is considered highly volatile when it moves up and down a lot.

The term 'shorting' is used to describe how traders sell the shares of a company when they believe or have made a bet that the company is worth less than what it's trading at. Bare shorting, meaning the seller has not borrowed the stock from a shareholder, is technically banned.

When 'shorters' get the story wrong, they often have to cover their position, meaning they have to buy back the shares. This can often result in sharp upward movements in share prices. Conversely, when shorters become active in a share, the price can fall based on seemingly no information. Shorters are active in most share markets; be mindful that a falling share might be the result of shorters, and they're not always correct. It's best to do your homework before reacting to a share price movement.

Share investing is completely different from trading. I recommend that you begin your share market journey as an investor. Investing is the process of buying a share for a longer period so that you receive the financial benefit of long-term price appreciation and dividend income. Share markets can be volatile – move up and down – so for optimal wealth creation, share investors will hold their shares for long periods of time, being mindful that adjustments along the way may be necessary.

These days, investors tend to hold their shares for shorter periods of time than they did historically, although the greatest wealth creation has been for those investors who have held the winning shares for decades. What makes a winning share will be outlined and explained in Chapter 4 and Chapter 7. The case studies in the appendix also provide more insight for those of you interested in more detail on selecting shares.

It's all in the timing

Time is the secret ingredient for share investors. Time allows for the magic of compounding to work. By reinvesting the income from shares in more shares and allowing the capital to grow, you accelerate the increase in the total value over time.

Let's say you save $500 every quarter and invest this money in shares at the end of the year: a $2000 investment.

Assuming the shares have appreciated on average 8 per cent p.a. and paid a constant 3.5 per cent dividend yield, your capital would grow to $5934 after ten years, assuming you reinvest your dividends.

Imagine if you invested an extra $1200 p.a. ($100 per month) each year for ten years, and reinvested the dividends, which remained at a constant 3.5 per cent yield.

- In current dollar terms, your $12,800 would increase to $28,000 after ten years.

- After 20 years, the investment would be worth $88,225.

- After 30 years, the investment would be worth $220,586.

- Over 40 years, the investment would be worth $507,500.

- Over 50 years, the investment would exceed $1 million.

By reinvesting the income from the dividends, you can reap the mathematical magic of compounding.

Savings and investing for the future can seem extremely abstract until the numbers come to life. Numbers don't lie. The more you invest now, the more financially sound you'll be in the future. If you're interested in calculating your own examples, there's an easy-to-use tool on Investopedia.com called the Dividend Investment Calculator.

When to start investing in shares

The younger you are when you start investing, the better opportunity you have for creating a sustainable future income stream, but shares are a great investment at any age. The best time to start investing in shares is now! You knew I was going to say that, didn't you?

If you're between 18 and 30

If you're in this younger age bracket, you have the benefit of time on your side. With as little as $500, you can invest to create a nest egg. Rather than putting cash in the bank, and being constantly tempted to spend it, investing in shares allows for greater savings – out of sight, out of mind. By drip-feeding even small amounts into investments and allowing the passage of time you'll create substantial growth in a pool of savings. A good way to do this is to allocate 10 per cent of your monthly pay packet to shares.

If you're not very patient, and saving for the future seems abstract, trading might be more appealing. If trading is your thing, be sure to start small and gain some experience before increasing your risk. Perhaps invest the majority of your money for the long term and put a little aside into a trading account for short-term trades.

If you're between 30 and 40

With a more stable career and full-time work comes the possibility of an annual bonus. Rather than taking the gold-plated holiday or buying the next best thing, invest your bonus shares for the future. Let patience be your friend. Thinking ahead is worthwhile, as you don't know what the future journey holds.

My peak earning period was between the ages of 23 and 38, as I then gave up my career to have my son. During that period, I aimed to save as much as I could to build my capital investment base.

If you're between 40 and 50

We all have to work longer, so saving for the future is important. Our spending and income is often challenged in this decade as family expenses can erode savings. At any opportunity, try to top up your savings to boost or start your share portfolio. Remember, cash in the bank offers little to no return. A share income at this stage of life is invaluable.

If you're between 50 and 60

Shares remain an extremely important asset for wealth creation as we age. This decade remains a very important period for maintaining shares. As the children grow up and the costs hopefully decrease, it's worth retaining a share portfolio and investing for the next life stage.

If you're over 60

As we age, our exposure to shares might decrease. Shares can be volatile and a sharp downward correction, like the 2008 crash, is harder for older investors as they may need the capital; a decline in value can erode financial security. Share prices do eventually recover but it's a long game.

To offset against this risk, financial advisers often recommend selling some shares and moving some cash into other financial instruments like corporate bonds, which have a lower risk profile. However, shares should remain part of your investment portfolio.

How to select shares

A multiplicity of investment firms analyse companies and share investments that are listed on the stock exchange, typically referred to as 'company research' or 'fundamental analysis' (Chapter 4). Traditionally, stockbrokers and investment banks were the primary research resources. The people who analyse the companies are not surprisingly called research analysts.

Companies are analysed on the basis of the profits (earnings) they generate each year and report to investors, a period known as the reporting season. Share prices will discount the future earnings expectations as forecast by analysts – more on this soon. In Australia, reporting season happens twice a year, with full-year and half-year results. Most companies have a June 30 year end; some have a March 31 year end. Company dividends (income) from the earnings are normally announced during the reporting periods, with the dividend amount as a percentage of the share price being referred to as the 'payout ratio'.

To compare companies, a like-for-like system was created, known as earnings per share or EPS. This is the earnings attributable to each share. The same type of calculation is applied to the dividends, known as dividends per share or DPS. I explore how to value and assess companies in more detail later, in Chapters 4 and 7.

The internet has enabled the creation of many more research sources to help investors make informed decisions. However, research on companies is usually not free. Investors, one way or another, will encounter a pay wall or a higher transaction cost to access the advice and recommendations.

There are many excellent online financial analysis websites for retail investors. Annual subscription fees vary. Free online content providers such as Livewire and FirstLinks offer commentary from professional investors and share market experts. Reading financial newspapers is another way to increase your general knowledge.

Chapter summary

- Shares are financial assets that you can buy through online share-trading platforms.

- Shares are suitable for any life stage and represent a low-cost, easy entry for investment to grow wealth and create an income.

- Interest rates will be lower for longer so cash on deposit is no longer such a lucrative savings vehicle.

- Shares allow for the mathematical magic of compounding to work.

- Shares are liquid and can be sold quickly and easily if you need to access your money.

- You can start share investing at any age, but time is an advantage, so the earlier the better.

- You can buy shares individually, or in groups with certain products such as ETFs or managed funds.

- Trading shares requires time and effort to watch the markets daily. Share investing is about buying good quality shares for the longer term.

3

The big and small economic picture: setting the stage for buying shares

Have you ever listened to a financial commentator on the TV or radio and wondered what on earth they were talking about? If you haven't studied economics, which most people haven't, it's not surprising that the language can seem like gobbledygook.

Shareplicity is all about keep things as simple as possible, but to understand the concepts in this book you do need to know some basic economic-speak. Even if you seek advice from an expert, you'll make better-informed decisions and create better money-making outcomes if you understand the basics of economics that I talk about in this chapter. You'll also protect yourself from having the wool pulled over your eyes, so to speak.

Economists have developed words, phrases and jargon to explain how economies work and what makes an economy expand and contract. Companies and shares are part of the economic equation; some general knowledge will improve your share investing skills.

When someone talks about 'macro-economics' they're talking about the big picture; 'micro-economics' is about the small economic picture. I look at each in turn in this chapter, then discuss how to interpret what they mean for share investing.

Understanding the macro-economic picture

Share investors can become bogged down in the details of what's called 'the macro picture'; a term used to describe what's happening in the Australian and global economies, what policies the central bankers have, and what avenues the federal and state governments are pursuing.

A central bank is basically the head bank of a country. It's the bank that controls the interest-rate settings for a country (called monetary policy) and for all the commercial banks (those you and I bank with). Central bankers are the men and women who administer the decisions of the central bank. In Australia, our central bank is known as the Reserve Bank of Australia (RBA). The USA has the Federal Reserve as its central bank. Central banks and governments have policies to grow economies and therefore, in theory, the profits of companies. They can also apply policies that are a risk to economies or parts of the economy and company profits.

Ultimately, the policies pursued will depend on how the economy is travelling based on consumer preferences and business confidence, manufacturing and export/import data, the construction industry, the housing market, levels of consumption and both price and wage growth.

The central bankers have been driving the policy agenda since the late 1970s. They have used interest rates as the levers to fire up economic growth or to temper inflation and therefore economic growth. Every time a slowdown or recession (a period of negative economic growth) hits, the central bankers lower rates. Then when inflation picks up they raise rates. It's like keeping a pot simmering, using just enough heat to keep the water bubbling, but not too much so the pot overflows.

Central bankers and the governor of the RBA aim for maximum employment and price stability. They don't like prices and wages rising too high or stagnating or falling, so they prefer inflation to be in the 2–3 per cent p.a. range.

Don't mention the 'R' word!

Australia was in the unique position of *not* having experienced a recession (when economic activity contracts and is negative for two consecutive quarters) for over 29 years. We bypassed the fall-out from the 2008 global financial crisis (GFC) for a number of reasons. However, as this book goes to press and global economies grapple with the spread of COVID-19, Australia's enviable record may come to a halt.

Recessions are not always inevitable, as can be seen from the sustained economic growth in both Australia and the USA since 2009; however, historically economies and company profits have moved in cycles. Upwards signifies a period of growth and expansion and downwards is a period of contraction. Figure 3.1 shows the cycle that has historically characterised our economy and the share market.

Share markets often replicate the highs and lows of the economic cycle, and that's why you'll hear so many experts say, 'Hold your shares for the long term to ride out the cycle'. Trying to time the cycles exactly – to sell at the top of the market and buy at the bottom – is challenging even for the most experienced investors.

The charts show that the cycles are neat and well defined but the theory doesn't often match reality, so I've found that it's best to err on the side of caution. I try not to rely too much on the concept of economic cycles when it comes to picking shares, because some shares can ride out a cycle and others can't.

Instead I focus on how to pick sustainable money-making shares. I give you some ideas for how to spot those shares that are more cyclically sensitive later in the book, in Chapters 4 and 5.

FIGURE 3.1: Economic cycles

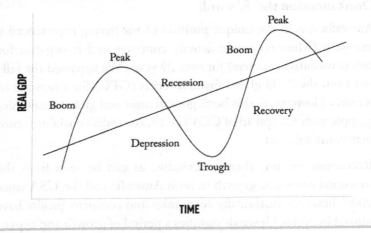

Macro-economic policies

There are two main macro-economic policies – monetary policy and fiscal policy.

Monetary policy is the term used to describe the tools that central banks use to change the interest rate settings; it's the cash rate in Australia and the federal or fed fund's rate in the USA. These tools can also regulate how much money is sloshing around in the economy.

Following the 2008 GFC, central bankers in the USA and Europe resorted to taking quantitative easing (QE) measures to boost growth in their economies. This means that they bought back financial instruments, like government bonds from banks, which in turn injected more cash into the system. Some people liken it to printing money!

Historically, more money in, and lower rates, means that it's cheaper and easier to borrow and invest, which allows consumers, investors and companies to invest and consume more.

Rules around monetary policy

- When central banks, like the RBA, cut interest rates, it's a positive for shares.

- Lower interest rates compared to other countries act to lower the currency value (the Australian dollar). Our government bonds that reflect the interest rate setting offer a lower yield (lower income for investors).

- Lower currency rates boost exporters (resource shares, like BHP) and shares that generate earnings from overseas (CSL, Resmed and James Hardie, for example).

- Conversely, when increase rates are raised, at some point it's a negative for share prices, because the cost of borrowing goes up and the income from shares isn't as attractive as popping the money in the bank. This holds true for companies and investors.

Fiscal policy is the domain of the politicians. It's often referred to as Keynesian policy after the economist John Maynard Keynes, who devised the strategy of governments boosting economic growth. Think 'jobs and growth', which was the catchphrase of one of our many former prime ministers.

Rules around fiscal policy

▸ Infrastructure spending is when governments spend money on public works such as roads, bridges and dams; this in turn injects money and jobs into the economy.

▸ The second way governments pull levers to increase economic growth is through lowering taxes (this is stimulatory); cutting so-called red tape and regulations and making it easier for companies to pursue profitable avenues, such as export incentives for mining companies.

▸ Last but hardly least is immigration. This has been a large driver for Australia and gives us one of the highest population growth rates in the developed world.

So, that's a great summary of the levers that can be used to change how an economy grows. Of course, it's never this simple in reality.

Don't try to outsmart the experts

Economists, those boffins and experts who spend hours analysing the economy for financial institutions, governments and non-government organisations (NGOs), often have conflicting views. It's amazing how many differing opinions exist at any point in time. For most investors, particularly when they're starting out, the commentary can be confusing and overwhelming – so it's easier to gravitate to well-known, longstanding commentators, right?

Of course, there's nothing wrong with listening to the 'experts', but they're not infallible. So, when the economic noise gets too loud, try not to focus on being an economic fortune-teller; instead, focus on the company in which you're investing.

Be prudent and keep an eye on interest rates, because the cost of money does have a direct bearing on the price of assets like shares, the type of shares you hold and how companies operate. A generally accepted view is that interest rates in Australia and around the world will stay lower for longer for many reasons, including ageing populations, an excess of savings, too much debt, overcapacity in manufacturing and the disruptive disinflationary impact of technology.

Also, avoid taking a stand against what the central banks are doing. A well-known expression for investors is 'Don't fight the Fed' (meaning the USA's Federal Reserve). Share prices move swiftly to align with the policies of a central bank; trying to outdo or outsmart the big bankers isn't a good idea for retail investors (that's you and me!).

Key takeaway points for the share investor

- Interest rates will be lower for longer, according to most Australian and world experts. This is favourable for shares.

- At some point governments, state and federal, will need to increase their fiscal spending on more infrastructure projects to boost economic growth. More money invested productively in the economy is good for companies and shares.

- Don't fight the big picture policies when buying shares.

Getting the gist of micro-economic factors

The micro-economic aspects are everything else that impacts on a company's earnings and therefore its shares. Here's a quick summary:

1. **Monopoly and oligopoly:** No, not the board game!
   A monopoly is when a company has 100 per cent market share and is the only operator (think Telstra pre-privatisation). An oligopoly occurs when a handful of companies compete against each other in a market. Australia's banks are an example. There are strict rules to stop oligopolistic behaviour that creates mutually beneficial outcomes, such as collusion of mortgage rate settings. However, some people would argue that it still happens.

2. **Sectors:** This is the term used to describe the environment in which a company operates. Some examples of market sectors are retail, building, banking and finance, and health care, which all have listed shares represented on the ASX (refer to Chapter 2). Also, I explore the sectors in more depth in Chapter 5, when I take you on the ASX 30 express.

   Sectors and sectoral themes are important when it comes to selecting managed funds and ETF products. These funds for indirect investors can focus solely on a sector, so you will need an understanding of what that means in terms of underlying shares and the outlook for the sector. There are many exciting themes outside of the traditional and historic areas that are now available for share investors.

3. **Competition:** Companies usually operate in a competitive market. Depending on the sector, the level of competition can vary. The greatest threat to a company, and therefore the shares you invest in, is competition. It can come in

many guises and is increasingly being felt by traditional businesses like banks, media and retail through the internet and technological disruption. You want to own shares in companies that can maintain or enhance their competitive edge without ruining profits; they're the winners for shareholders. The competitive edge is often referred to as a moat – a metaphorical depiction of the protection the company has against the enemy (competitors).

4. **Sales and revenue (the top line):** Depending on the sector, the amount a company registers in products sold or services rendered will be reported as sales or revenue in its annual report. Shareholders need to be on the lookout for percentage differences from the previous year and whether the rate of change is slowing or accelerating. In the current low growth world, you want your shares to grow the top line by 10 per cent or more if possible, without hurting margins and profit (more about those following). The larger the company, the harder it can be to grow the top line. For example, a sale valued at $100 for a company with only $2000 in revenue has a considerably higher impact on growth than a company with $100 million in revenue.

5. **Margins:** These are the percentage amounts that determine how profitable a company is. They will change depending on the costs of the business. Companies can be grouped into two distinct categories:

   High volume (top-line)/low-margin growth businesses: examples are discount retailers like Kmart that work on boosting sales revenue with cheaper priced goods and a no-frills store. The margins are tighter (smaller) because they make their money from high volume sales.

Lower volume/higher margin businesses: look no further than Ferrari, which has small run rates of cars produced at very high prices.

Share investors like shares where margins can expand: higher margins normally equals higher earnings, which equals better shareholder returns and better money-making opportunities. Contracting margins, conversely, aren't good for shares.

6. **Profit:** This is what you want to see as a shareholder: a company that can grow profits. Higher profits equal more potential for the share price to go up, and therefore the higher the amount of dividend payment you may receive.

Traditionally, companies have not sought government intervention when it comes to aspects of micro-economic policies, unless of course it generates higher profits (such as deregulation in the late 1980s and 1990s, which reduced red tape). However, markets and self-regulation are being increasingly scrutinised as having fault lines, leaving investors exposed. Problems with rising electricity prices and concern about low mortgage rates, for example, have brought politics into the sphere of shares. As you discover more about what kind of shares will make you money, this will become apparent; the companies that can navigate government policy and regulation will be the best choices for making good money and you being able to sleep at night.

Companies aim to make profits, which in turn makes you, the shareholder, money. Making profits at any cost is becoming less acceptable in the 21st century, as it allows for risk-taking behaviour that can be detrimental to shareholders' earnings. A recent example was undetected money laundering activities within the operations of some of Australia's banks. Both Westpac and Commonwealth Bank shares fell sharply and suffered from the public fallout of money laundering charges.

Increasingly, shareholders large and small are requiring companies to not only be more accountable to their equity investors (people like us) but to the world in which they operate. This investment trend is known as sustainable and/or environmental, social and governance (ESG). Even if this doesn't hold any interest for you, there's undeniably a global push in this direction for major investment houses. In Chapter 6, I explain the risks and opportunities for investors in the 21st century, as fortunes will be made and lost along the way.

Learning from the lessons of history

Driving while looking through the rear vision mirror is dangerous because the road behind doesn't define the road ahead. The same goes for share investing – what has worked in the past may not work in the future. A number of major macro- and micro-economic trends are at work in this third decade of the 21st century, largely because of the advancement in computing technology and the internet. These trends are important to share investors because companies are at risk from disruption and the changing patterns of investors and consumers – just look at the problems Netflix has created for free-to-air television and the opportunities smartphones have provided for both traditional and new businesses.

As the younger generations embrace the change, the way in which they consume also changes; their lifestyles and aspirations are changing the markets. The shares you might have bought in the past are no longer the best options to make you money.

The rate of change is accelerating in the world. The change is obvious, but not all new companies will successfully capitalise on innovation, disruption and the emerging growth markets of Generation Z. Some of the older companies, the so-called household names, may shrink in relevance and become smaller.

Whether you're new to the share market or a seasoned investor, I want you to retain an open mind and the ability to think differently. You can make lots of money if you can successfully identify the next big company. You can only do this by being open minded and changing your perspective and view of the world. Accept that what worked in the past may not necessarily determine how you invest for the future.

Macro- and micro-economic trends that can affect future share investment

► Disruption from technology; geographic borders no longer provide a defence from overseas competition.

► Changing consumer tastes from Gen Z and the millennial generation.

► Challenges to traditional business models by shareholder activism, the emergence of increased governance, environmental and social pressures – think Westpac and Commonwealth Bank money laundering.

► Populism, trade wars and climate change.

How investors analyse the share market

Now you have some insight into the macro- and micro-economic pictures, you can start to understand how investors analyse the share market and select companies with the best profit-generating ideas. They do this in two ways:

1. top-down approach

2. bottom-up approach.

Top-down approach to investing: watching share market sectors

The top-down approach is used extensively by professional investors. They look at the big picture – at sectors and economies – to see how well companies and shares exposed to the current market will do and whether this means an increase in earnings.

For example, a professional share manager for an actively managed fund might say, 'We like the top-down fundamentals of XYZ sector nationally or globally and we recommend you buy the largest companies in that sector'. Or they might say: 'Interest rates are being cut in Australia, and that means a more favourable outlook for the housing market, both in terms of boosting new dwelling construction and the existing dwelling market. In turn, we recommend shares in Boral and REA as two examples that will benefit from the improved market conditions'. Boral is one of Australia's largest building material suppliers – concrete, cement, and timber products; REA is the premier online real estate portal in Australia to advertise properties to buy/sell and rent.

Another example of a top-down approach is when a research analyst recommends you buy BHP and Rio Tinto (RIO) shares because they think China is investing more in infrastructure and it's very positive for steel production and therefore iron ore, which these mining giants produce.

Bottom up: watching shares

A bottom-up approach is the opposite and refers to the direct analysis and selection of shares based on the favourable criteria that will make the share price rise. If someone had said two years ago that the younger generation would be using payment systems called Afterpay or Zip instead of a debit or credit card, you would have laughed.

Afterpay and Zip are just two of the many new payment platforms that allow shoppers to use technology to provide the good old-fashioned lay-by. These two companies' shares prices have skyrocketed in response to the huge demand for the payment platforms from consumers and retailers/vendors.

Afterpay's share price is up over 100 per cent in a year and Zip's is up 200 per cent. These results have been achieved during a period when a top-down analysis could have misled you, the share investor. Sluggish retail sales might have put you off buying companies involved in payment platforms. You could have easily reasoned that it was too risky to buy shares in new companies that offer a different payment system.

What many investors, including some professional investors, failed to realise is that shoppers love lay-by. They can register and buy online or in store and pay just a quarter of the value of the purchase, take their purchase home, then pay the remaining three-quarters off in monthly instalments. Afterpay and Zip offer instant shopper gratification, with no interest costs and no risk of going into credit card debt. These business models have been successful despite a poor retail backdrop by taking market share from other payment platforms.

Which approach is best?
The moral of the investment story is that both options – looking at share market sectors and looking at shares – can provide opportunities and misleading signals when it comes to buying shares. After years of share investing, I have concluded that the top-down approach is far less valuable to the likes of you and me. We don't need to compare our share market investments to an index like professional investors do. We do, however, want to make money in an absolute not relative sense.

The bottom-up approach helps me to focus on a company and the opportunities for the share. I can't tell you how many times I've taken the wrong path to share purchases from the top down, without paying enough attention to the bottom-up analysis. I give you an example in the case study about the engineering company RCR Tomlinson in the appendix.

In Chapter 8, I reveal why the passive ETF market is growing so strongly. The top-down approach for ETFs can be a winning strategy; however, knowing what you're buying is also important. For example, a country ETF may seem like a good idea, but on closer inspection, the major companies in the ETF may not be what you want to hold. In Australia, the major companies might be the financials (banks and insurance) and resource shares (materials and energy), as they represent a large proportion of the country index, which is reflected in the ETF.

Living in a low-interest-rate world

In the current economic climate, cash in the bank is not earning interest and the temptation to spend it out of frustration can be high! What if I told you that there can be and has been a share which has turned people like you into millionaires? The following are two good examples of how important compounding and growth are in our low-interest-rate and low-growth world. The past returns of Commonwealth Bank (CBA) and CSL can't be guaranteed in the future, of course, but they are indicative of the money-making opportunities available in share investing.

Commonwealth Bank

If you bought the minimum amount of 480 shares in CBA's 1991 initial public offering (IPO) at a price of $4.50 ($2160), they would be worth $43,200 at the current price of $90 per share.

Over the 29 years, Commonwealth Bank has paid out dividends of $31,680, giving a total return of $74,880 if the shares were sold and the capital gain (profit) realised, making a 3475 per cent total return (capital gain and dividends) over a 28-year period. Depending on your tax position, the total return could also have been boosted by franking credits, as Commonwealth Bank pays a 100 per cent franked dividend. (Franked dividends are explained in Chapters 2 and 7 and summarised in the glossary.)

CSL

In 1994 the company CSL – originally called Commonwealth Serum Laboratories and part of the CSIRO – was sold out of CSIRO by the government to the public as a developing biotech company. The minimum 400 parcel of shares at the IPO price of $2.30 equalled a $920 investment. In October 2007, CSL had a 3-for-1 share split, meaning the 400 shares became 1200 shares. At the current price of $330 at time of writing, your shareholding would be worth $396,000. Dividends paid over the period to the March 2020 dividend would equal $20,899.08. If you sold the shares, the total return would be $416,899 – you would have made almost 450 times what you invested.

If you'd bought 1200 CSL shares at the IPO, at a cost of $2760, you would now own 3600 shares valued at $1,188,000 excluding dividends.

By comparison, $3000 held as cash in the bank at a compound interest rate of 5 per cent would have delivered just over $10,000 over the same 25-year period. Interest rates are even lower now, and growth rates are more challenged. Therefore, our mission, should we choose to accept it, is to find those shares that can offer us real money-making opportunities. Not all companies are like CSL, but they do exist. Amazon, Apple and Microsoft have been huge wealth creators and some experts claim Tesla will one

day be the next eye-popping millionaire factory for share investors. In Australia, shares including those in a2 Milk, Afterpay
and Macquarie Bank have created wealth for investors in a short
space of time.

Note: I include discussions about some of these companies and
their shares in case studies in the appendix, which you can flick
over to at any time.

Chapter summary

- Monetary policy controls interest rates and the amount of cash
  in the financial system. Central banks set a country's monetary
  policy.

- Fiscal policy is set by governments.

- Interest rates up = generally a negative for shares.

- Interest rates down = generally a positive for shares.

- Australia and the world have entered a great period of change.
  Invest with an open mind and be receptive to threats and
  opportunities.

- Australia and the world will experience lower interest rates for
  longer. Shares offer better returns than cash on deposit.

- Remember the magic of compounding and growth to help your
  savings make you money.

- Keep it simple and block out the noise.

- Top-down recommendations are okay, but don't forget the
  bottom-up aspect.

4

Deciding which shares to buy

If you've watched the 1987 film *Wall Street*, with all the glitz and the glamour of the 'greed is good' 1980s, you could be forgiven for thinking that stockbroking is a boozy, male-dominated affair, with people buying and selling shares on tips and whispers and making millions of dollars! However, that's the movies, remember? It's not like that in real life.

You've probably also heard about research experts in investment banks and other firms crunching numbers and calculating ratios. They're looking at a company's fundamentals. This is called fundamental analysis; sounds fancy, I know, but it's simply about deciding which shares to buy.

Share markets are not perfect. Like the companies and people that run them, nothing is certain, so we use fundamental analysis and financial ratios to improve our decision-making.

In this chapter, I show you how to identify which of the 2300 shares listed on the Australian stock exchange will make you money, the red flags that indicate potential capital killers and criteria for picking the winners from the losers. You don't have to become an expert but you do need to understand the key issues so that you make money as well as not lose money. I show you how to do just enough research to achieve the results you want. So, let's start with the fundamentals.

Defining fundamental analysis

I find the easiest way to explain the basics of fundamental analysis is to refer to your own personal situation.

- **Revenue:** This is how much you earn from your salary or wages.

- **Costs:** These include your income tax; living costs (food, utilities); rent or paying off your mortgage; lifestyle costs (holidays and entertainment); investing in yourself by studying or training; and the cost of paying down debt – interest on your mortgage or credit card debts or personal loans.

- **Profit:** This is the difference between your revenue and costs. If it's a positive number you might treat yourself (which is like a company paying shareholders a dividend); or you might reinvest it (buy a bigger house, pay for more study, buy some shares); or you might pay down more debt, which will save you in interest costs.

- **Cash flow:** This is your ability to pay your bills in the future. Will your circumstances change?

At the end of the day, what matters most to us and our personal finances is the cash flow we have after all costs. This is what allows us to grow our assets, reduce our borrowings and/or invest for our future. Most of us come unstuck when we gather too much debt and we can't pay it off, or we spend too much of our cash flow trying to reduce our debt.

For all intents and purposes, companies operate in the same way, just on a much larger scale, in more complex businesses. Companies, people and economies all operate on a cash-in and cash-out basis. The good businesses are those that can sustainably maximise the cash in (revenue) to make a return to shareholders via profits and dividends. This increases the share price because this is the type of company investors are interested in. Did you notice that I used the word 'sustainably'? This is because we want these results without ripping off stakeholders (think workers, customers, suppliers and the environment).

As outlined in the story about Ford Motor Company in Chapter 1, companies are about people, egos and corporate culture. The shares that represent the underlying company, however, are judged on the financial fundamentals.

This analysis creates a platform to compare one share against another to determine which shares offer the best money-making opportunities.

Doing the research: key financial statistics

Most investors have neither the time, energy nor inclination to commit to analysing the financial statements of every company on the stock exchange. Also, spending hours on analysis doesn't secure the best share market outcomes. However, it's important that you understand a few key financial statistics and ratios and what they mean when it comes to buying and selling shares.

You don't need to spend hours poring over financial data. Your job to is learn what to look for, not how to be the research expert.

If you run your own business, you'll be familiar with the following three key reports that give you insights into how your company is performing:

1. the profit and loss (P&L) statement

2. the balance sheet

3. the cash flow statement.

As investors, we need to rely on the quality of disclosure in these three financial statements, which companies publish in their annual, half-yearly and sometimes quarterly reports. The key financial statistics, which help us determine how financially robust a company is, are calculated from these financial statements. If you subscribe to an online broker such as CommSec, these key financial statistics are summarised for you. Online share information services or your share broker usually offer the same service.

In the following section, I show you how to read the financial statistics of two Australian shares, Aristocrat Leisure and Speedcast International. Both companies have expanded their businesses through acquisitions, financed mostly through borrowings. One company has been very successful and been a money-maker for shareholders and the other is what I call a capital killer – a 'dog' or a loser! How do I know this? I own shares in one of the companies and have done so for a while, and thankfully I recognised the capital killer and sold before I lost money.

Aristocrat Leisure

Let's look at Aristocrat first. Figure 4.1 and Table 4.1 depict a numerical summary of the trends that help you to identify shares that will make you money. Please note that it's the trends that are important, as a company's financials (revenue, profits and so on) can be lumpy due to an acquisition.

FIGURE 4.1: Four-year summary of Aristocrat's financial picture

Income Statement   Quarterly   Annual

2019 (Millions AUD)	
● Revenue	4,397.40
● Net Income	698.80
● Profit Margin	15.89%

Balance Sheet   Quarterly   Annual

2019 (Millions AUD)	
● Total Assets	6,337.00
● Total Liabilities	4,193.40
● Debt to Assets	44.07%

Cash Flow   Quarterly   Annual

2019 (Millions AUD)	
● Operating	1,085.50
● Investing	-337.40
● Financing	-607.60

Source: Bloomberg

Key ratios and trends in Figure 4.1 that matter for you when looking at a share to buy are:

► Revenue is trending upwards.

► Net income (profits) is trending upwards.

► Net profit margins suffered after some acquisitions in 2017–18, but by 2019, the uptrend had returned as the acquisitions contributed to earnings.

- Debt, although increasing due to the acquisitions, as a percentage of total assets is below 100 per cent; in this case 44 per cent is a very reasonable level.

- In 2019 operating cash flow comfortably covered the investing and financing cash flow obligations – those are the funds needed to run the business, pay interest and keep it growing.

TABLE 4.1: Four-year summary of Aristocrat's key balance sheet items

Aristocrat	2016	2017	2018	2019
Long-term debt ($m)	1288	1199	2881	2793
Net interest cover (x)	6.63	14.71	9.23	9.40
Net gearing (%)	93.4	48.5	141.6	103.8

Source: Aristocrat Annual Report

Key points from Table 4.1 that matter for you when looking at a share to buy are:

- Long-term debt has more than doubled to fund the acquisitions.

- Net interest cover, meaning earnings before interest and tax (EBIT), covers the level of interest costs by a factor of 9.40x. This means the company can cope with either a fall in earnings or an increase in interest costs and it will not be detrimental to shareholders.

- Net gearing means long-term debt less cash is 103.8 per cent of shareholders' funds. This is a decline of 27%, a trend in the right direction.

Aristocrat is a great example of a company that has successfully managed to increase its long-term debt, while still managing to generate sufficient income and cash flow to cover the interest costs and make net profit. Companies have two ways to grow – organically (via existing operations, cutting costs or investment from cash flow) or via acquisitions. Good companies can navigate the pathways to growth. When this happens shareholders make money!

FIGURE 4.2: Aristocrat share price over the last four years

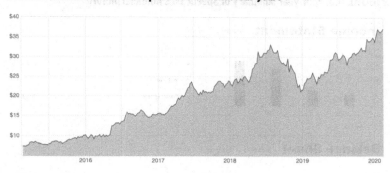

Source: Marketindex.com.au

A share price that trends from the bottom left corner to the top right over the long term (as shown in Figure 4.2) flags a share you want to own. Share prices do not always move in a straight line, of course, for many reasons. In the Aristocrat example, the company invested heavily in acquisitions to grow the business for the future. This investment increased its interest-bearing debt and reduced the interest cover. As the share market discounts future earnings, it was concerned that the acquisitions would not be so positive to earnings, and the shares were correspondingly sold down. However, as the results for 2019 came forth, it became clearer to investors that the acquisitions would boost earnings, profits and thus the share price. In the next chapter, this will become clearer when I discuss the earnings' forecasts for Aristocrat.

Speedcast International

Speedcast International also expanded by buying more businesses, and funded the acquisitions through debt and an equity issue (it raised more cash by issuing – selling – more shares). However, Speedcast's operations were not as successful in generating the cash flow needed from new acquisitions.

FIGURE 4.3: Four-year summary of Speedcast's financial picture

Source: Bloomberg

Key points from Figure 4.3 that matter for you when looking at a share to buy are:

- Revenue for Speedcast grew substantially but net profit margin (how profitable the business is) declined to an unsustainable 0.3%. This is a bad sign for investors.

- Net income correspondingly fell; also bad for investors.

The fall in income meant Speedcast was forced to issue three profit warnings: first in late December 2018, again in July 2019 and most recently in early February 2020, when the shares were placed in a three-week trading halt – meaning you're unable to buy or sell the shares on the stock market. A company issues these types of requests to the stock exchange when there is price-sensitive information and it wants to ensure nothing is leaked to the market until all shareholders can be in receipt of the information. The share price fell correspondingly, as a reaction to the lower profits. Shareholders don't want a profit warning and will normally sell the shares when one is issued. A company that consistently issues profit warnings is a sell in my opinion. Once, twice, maybe – but three times is an ominous signal.

TABLE 4.2: Four-year summary of Speedcast's key balance sheet items

Speedcast	2015	2016	2017	2018
Long-term debt (US$m)	99	368	432	625
Net interest cover (x)	1.85	1.31	0.31	0.21
Net gearing (%)	309.5	119.2	123.2	195.8

Source: Speedcast Annual Report

Key points from Table 4.2 that matter for you when looking at a share to buy are:

- Long-term debt for Speedcast increased by over six times in a four-year period – a warning sign.
- Interest cover fell by over 80 per cent – another big warning sign that all isn't going well with the business.
- In November 2016, Speedcast raised $295 million from issuing new shares; this is what accounts for the fall in the net gearing. This means shareholders' funds increased relative to the debt. Regrettably, by 2018 net gearing had almost doubled. This is another problem; at almost 200 per cent it's far too high.

FIGURE 4.4: Speedcast share price over the last four years

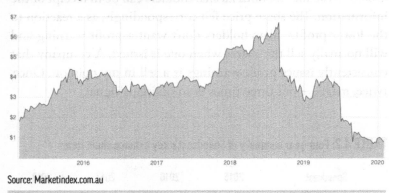

Source: Marketindex.com.au

Figure 4.4 tells two stories about Speedcast. After the 2018 results, investors were optimistic that the company would do a lot better and make a lot more profits from the acquisitions. However, as the business spluttered and the fault lines appeared, earnings were cut and the share price correspondingly fell from almost $7 in mid-2019 to around $0.70 currently. This isn't the picture of a share you want to own.

Look for the red flags

The Aristocrat versus Speedcast case is a good example of how quickly the wheels can fall off when a company pursues an aggressive expansion strategy and profits don't grow sufficiently or, in this case, actually fall, risking the financial security of the company. This is an example of how a company can go broke! In a worst-case scenario, assets can't be sold fast enough or more money raised, so the share price can go to zero. It doesn't happen very often, but none of us want to be caught in a downdraft of a share under pressure due to cash flow problems.

Remember, companies need to invest to grow earnings. Companies that fail to invest risk failing to provide good share market returns. Of course, not all investment and acquisitions work out, and some Australian companies have been more successful than others in expanding overseas. The point of these financial ratios is to highlight that you need to look at a company's cash flow and balance sheet as well as the earnings.

Red flags for share investors are as important as the great money-making ideas. Profit downgrades, falling earnings and rising debt can all erode the share price. It's always about the cash flow, and when not enough is being generated to cover all the costs then you, the shareholder, will suffer.

Share prices can rise indefinitely for good companies over many years, and other companies just don't make it.

What makes shareholders money?

Two financial ratios, calculated from the earnings a company generates, are used universally and provide a basis of valuing shares for investors. These are the two that you need to observe and understand to assist you to make the optimal share purchases:

1. Earnings per share (EPS) – this is an allocation of how much net profit is attributed to each share.

2. Dividend per share (DPS) – the actual cash payment the shareholder receives, normally twice a year.

For most of us, EPS is quite an abstract concept. Here's a good analogy: a vigneron plants a grapevine. The vine isn't planted with the expectation that the vine and the grape harvest will stay the same as time progresses. Each year the vigneron works at enabling the vine to grow more stalks and stems, and with each new stalk and stem, more grapes will be produced.

The growth in the stalks and the stems are the EPS growth, so to speak, and the grapes yielded are the DPS.

It's the same for a share: you aim to buy shares that deliver good growth in earnings (vine stalks and stems) so that you receive a higher value for the vineyard based on the higher production capacity. Along the way the higher dividends (the grape harvest) deliver the income gained from holding the share.

Earnings per share

Earnings per share is the net profit divided by the number of shares listed on the stock exchange. It's important as it provides the basic number that's compared to the share price to value the share.

You want shares that can grow their EPS consistently. As the earnings grow, the share price appreciates in value, reflecting the higher EPS.

Conversely, when the EPS falls (which it can, as in the Speedcast example), the share price will also fall. That isn't what you want.

Dividend per share

The DPS is the amount paid to each shareholder out of the EPS. It's the reward for shareholders who invest in the company and is paid twice a year. Unlike the share price rise for growing the EPS, the DPS is real cash in the bank. EPS is capital gain and dividends are income.

The dividend is important for investors who want an income from their shares. Dividend payments also provide a solid buffer for you when share markets fall. You'll often hear commentators referring to the benefits of dividends when share markets are going down or flatlining or moving sideways.

Dividends are paid at the discretion of the management and board of the company. In the case of Speedcast (see the previous section) they suspended the dividend for shareholders in 2019 because the company did not have enough money.

However, dividends are not a 'right' for shareholders. So, should you buy shares for the dividend only (income) or for the capital appreciation in the share price (known as growth)?

The answer is, it depends on you! What do you want from your shares? It often depends on what stage you're at in your life. For example, if you're retired you might rely on dividend income to live; if you're younger you may want to buy shares that pay a low to zero dividend because they're growing the EPS so strongly.

Some investors often see it as an either/or scenario, but the truth is that it's always better to invest in a share with some dividend payment.

Chapters 5 and 7 explain how you can pick the dividend champions and why they're so important for creating long-term wealth. In these chapters, I also discuss why investors who chase dividends only can be disappointed when the capital invested falls. Australian share investors benefitted for many years from a high income on some of the most popular shares. However, this strategy has become more complicated because of a changing regulatory and competitive market.

Key ratios used to value shares

Now you have knowledge of the basic financials of a share and what makes you money, you can use the price of the share to calculate specific mathematical ratios to provide an indication of the value of the share. Is it cheap or expensive? Even if it's a great investment, you don't want to pay too much for it in the short term!

The two go-to ratios that you need to understand are the price to earnings ratio (PER) and the dividend yield.

Price to earnings ratio

The PER (sometimes called P/E ratio) equals the price of the share divided by the EPS. The PER is a measurement ratio defined by 'x', meaning times. It's a standard measurement to establish whether a share is cheap or expensive, and its value relative to other shares.

Here's a simple example.

If the share price is $10 and the EPS is $1, then the PER is 10x.

This means it will take ten years to pay off the cost of the share in terms of the EPS you make each year. The higher the EPS growth, the more quickly your share investment is paid off.

Using the grapevine example from earlier, the quicker the vine grows and the more grapes produced, the faster your original capital outlay is recouped and the more valuable the vineyard is to a potential buyer. Some people, particularly those looking for income rather than growth, pick a benchmark and won't consider a share with a PER of more than 15x, for example. They are often referred to as 'value investors'.

Others have a different approach and believe that in a low-interest-rate world, growth in earnings and a lower dividend are more important for making money – the share price will rise considerably more and the dividend payments are not so important. The future rise in the share price, which will translate into a profit when they eventually sell their shares, will more than offset the income from dividends over the same period. This is often called 'growth investing' and many growth shares trade on high PER multiples.

Chapters 5, 6 and 7 delve more deeply into the concepts of value, growth and dividend investing, as well as what shares have been the money-makers for investors.

Industry valuation terms

Table 4.3 offers some insight into the depth of valuation terms used in the investing industry. Valuing companies is fraught with differing opinions and very much determined through the eye of the beholder or buyer/seller and the context the company finds itself in.

It's rational to buy shares as described in columns 1–4 and try to 'bag a bargain'. However, because of unconscious biases and herd mentality it's easy to become caught up in the moment of rising share prices and greed and end up buying shares as described in columns 5–7, sometimes even in column 8!

TABLE 4.3: The spectrum of valuation terms for share investing – red, amber and green

1	2	3	4	5	6	7	8
Rock bottom	Cheap	Undervalued	Fairly valued	Fully valued	Overvalued	Expensive	Bubble-like territory
Completely bombed out – no buyers, possibly a bargain or could be a trap. Like discounted food that may be going off sooner than you anticipated	Looks cheap though not a bargain; let's say a 20% sale off the retail price, not 50%	Lower than what is considered the intrinsic value	Like Goldilocks and the three bears: not too hot and not too cold – just right. You are paying for what you receive in the current investment environment	You are paying more for what you receive	Potentially over-paying	Definitely over-paying, particularly on a near-to short-term time horizon	Extremely over-priced and could result in a bursting (price collapse)
Red lights flashing warning	Amber to green light	Some amber but more green	Green lights	Green to amber lights	Amber to red light	More red than amber	Red lights flashing warning

I've colour referenced the different value terms in the last row of the table, in an attempt to give you some feeling for when there are risks in valuations, with 'risk' defined as the chance of losing money: rock bottom and bubble-like territory both come with a red flag. When a share appears ridiculously cheap, there is usually a reason for this – perhaps the company is going bust. At the other end of the spectrum, remember that bubbles always burst!

Generally speaking, any PER multiple (in the current low-interest-rate environment) of 15-17x is probably the 'fairly valued' segment, with any lower PER falling in the left columns of the table and any higher PER in the right. However, you need to be careful using such absolutes. PER multiples only tell half of the story; the PER and dividend yield should always be considered within the context of the share (see Chapter 5).

Share price targets

You may hear commentators talk about the 'share price target'; for example, 'The share price target for Company X is $300 and the current share price is $250'. What does this mean? The target can be higher or lower than the real price, and changes depending on the EPS forecast.

Just because an analyst or commentator creates a share price target, it doesn't literally mean the real price will move to that target. Sometimes the price will move more or less than the target. That's what makes the market. Share price targets are an indication of future movement but not a guaranteed outcome. Don't be fooled, as analysts change targets depending on changes in earnings forecasts. When the EPS forecast is growing – i.e. profits are forecast to increase – the share price target also increases; and vice versa, à la Speedcast, the EPS falls and the share price falls. EPS can change based on any number of factors, such as improved earnings or a hit to profits due to an extreme event or the 2020 coronavirus. Targets are used to give investors an expectation of where the share price can move to in the future.

During reporting season, when companies announce the half-year or full-year earnings results, analysts often change the earnings forecasts and the share price targets, up or down. It goes without saying: you want to be holding the shares that the analysts upgrade, not downgrade. A downgrade results in the share price falling, not indefinitely but until the share has moved to a better valuation, becoming fairly valued or less.

Targets are a good indicator of what's possible in terms of the share price movements. It's often preferable to look at the average (consensus) share price target (supplied by some online share services) rather than a one-off target. That's because the analysts' forecasts can vary quite considerably. This is what creates a market; differing opinions mean sellers and buyers, although sometimes everyone moves like a herd (more on this in Chapter 6).

Share price targets are often the reference point upon which analysts and share market commentators relate whether a share is cheap or expensive, as per Table 4.3. If a share is trading below the share price target, it can be referred to by any of the terms from 'fairly valued' to 'rock bottom'. Conversely, if a share price is trading above the share price target, it can be referred to by any of the terms from 'fairly valued' to 'bubble-like'.

Analysts also use the terms 'underweight' and 'overweight' to indicate whether they consider the share to offer money-making opportunities or the potential to not do so well. 'Underweight' is a soft way of saying sell or don't hold the index weighting of the share. 'Overweight' is the opposite and is a soft way of saying the equities analyst thinks the shares are worth holding, even above the index weighting. The shares may not be an outright buy at the time of the recommendation, but an 'overweight' indicates 'do not sell' or 'buy more if the share price falls'.

Dividend yield

This is the annual DPS divided by the share price. If the DPS is $0.40 and the share price is $10 then the yield is 4 per cent. This is the income (reward) you receive as a shareholder for buying the share.

Assuming DPS stays the same, if the share price goes up, the dividend yield will fall. The opposite happens when the share price falls, assuming the DPS stays the same. All dividends are dependent on the earnings, so any deterioration in earnings or fall may result in a cut in the dividend. A dividend isn't a sacred cow.

In our low-interest-rate world, you would be wise to remain sceptical of shares that trade on a dividend yield above 5 per cent as a general rule. Higher yielding shares can often be a harbinger of a dividend cut and potential share price fall. Remember: if it sounds too good to be true, then it could well be the case.

Chapter summary

- ► Share market fundamentals include the key financial statistics that are used to spot the winners and the losers: revenue, income, margins, debt, cashflow and gearing.

- ► Spot the red flags for the capital killers: look at a company's cash flow and balance sheet as well as its earnings.

- ► Earnings per share (EPS) and dividend per share (DPS) are important valuation measures to consider when buying shares.

- ► Use the price to earnings ratio (PER) and the dividend yield to value shares and compare them: are they cheap or expensive?

- ► The red, amber and green valuation table offers insight into the valuation terms used for shares.

- ► A share price target is an analyst's indication of where a share price may move to in the future.

5

Looking at Australia's biggest shares

In share market circles, investors often argue about whether value investing or growth investing is better. (I mentioned these in the section on PER in Chapter 4.)

Value investors buy 'cheap' shares; let's say on a PER multiple ranging from single digits to maybe 17x at the absolute most. These cheap shares offer a dividend yield of 4–6 per cent and may not have been the best share price performers.

Growth investors, on the other hand, look for long-term secular growth that is normally equated with a higher PER multiple, sometimes at eye-watering levels of 50x plus, and nil to little dividend income to shareholders. 'Secular' refers to consistent, long-term growth trends in markets unaffected by short-term trends: these days for example computers, mobile phones and the internet. Railroads and the gasoline motor car were the secular markets of the 20th century. This type of investing may have been helped by very low interest rates.

Shares are often lumped into these two categories, which I believe is clumsy and potentially misleading for most of us as it's too simplistic and means investors can miss out on significant money-making shares.

In this chapter, I tease out some subtleties for you. The expression 'lies, damned lies and statistics' is a reminder that numbers in isolation can be misleading about what's really happening. The duck might be paddling hard under the water to stay afloat, when on the surface the water is smooth.

When it comes to analysing shares, you need to look a little deeper into what the numbers are saying, in conjunction with the type of business the companies are operating, before coming to a conclusion. You need to do your research to provide some context to the ratios.

In this chapter, I take you on the ASX 30 express: a bus stop tour of Australia's top 30 shares at the time of writing. I explain how the PER and dividend yield vary, what makes some shares different and how you can make money. The best way to understand shares and what makes money is to refer to real life examples. Then you can put all your newly acquired knowledge into practice.

Catching the ASX 30 share express

Come on a journey with me on the ASX 30 share express bus. At each stop I'll explain the characteristics that define the shares.

Each bus stop will list the shares in groups, with the current share price, the forecast 2020 PER, the forecast dividend yield and the analyst share price target (see note). The bus stops (groups) I have created are not strictly the sectors they're categorised in by the ASX (refer to Chapter 2). Some of the groups correspond to the correct sectors, but try not to get too bogged down in the details.

All the figures were compiled at the close of business on 14 February 2020. Share prices are fluid, so the numbers will be different in the future, but the themes will remain the same.

Note: The data for the ASX 30 express has been sourced from FNArena (FNArena.com). The EPS, DPS and share price targets are based on the consensus figures collated from stock research used for the FNArena database. The share price targets move up and sometimes down as the forecasts change (usually around reporting season), but are based on the prospective EPS and DPS forecasts – they're not historical. The ASX 30 is designed as illustrative rather than absolutely definitive and investors should conduct their own research before buying or selling shares, as data and share prices move constantly.

First stop: mining, energy and resources

TABLE 5.1: Your first seven shares – value and cyclical stocks

Code	Company	Sector	Share price	2020 PER	2020 yield	Share price target
BHP	BHP Group	Mining & Energy	$38.65	12.6x	5.20%	$39.58
STO	Santos	Energy/Gas	$8.19	15.7x	2.30%	$8.73
WPL	Woodside Petroleum	Energy/LNG	$32.83	16.2x	4.80%	$35.98
FMG	Fortescue Metals	Mining/Iron Ore	$10.99	5.6x	20.40%	$9.64
S32	South32	Mining/Coal	$2.63	35.9x	2.10%	$2.91
RIO	Rio Tinto	Mining/Iron Ore	$97.65	10.3x	7.60%	$100.34
NCM	Newcrest Mining	Gold & Silver	$27.99	20.2x	1.00%	$28.00

Source: FNArena

In Table 5.1, you can see from the forecast PER and dividend yield that there's a quite a large disparity in the size of the numbers: the PER is as low as 5.6x for Fortescue and as high as 20.2x for Newcrest Mining and yet all of these shares are termed 'value'. You're probably thinking that makes no sense at all – value is meant to be cheap with a low PER. The problem is that the tag 'value' fails to explain to the investor that these shares derive their revenue and profits from cyclical commodity markets, meaning that the earnings can go up and down markedly over time as the demand and supply shifts for their products.

For example, iron ore prices are relatively high, so Australia's three major low-cost iron ore producers – BHP, Rio and Fortescue – are making heaps of money and generating so much cash that they can pay out big dividends. Yippee, you think: buy, buy, buy. However, as the share price target suggests (because it's below the real share price, for Fortescue) along with the high yield, the expert analysts don't believe the high iron ore prices will last. Uncertainty around the impacts of the coronavirus has created further price fluctuations. Should that forecast turn out to be right, you'd be buying a fully priced share that could suffer from a profit downgrade and a cut in the dividend in the future, which could lead to share price falls and both an income and capital loss.

Conversely, South32, which is a coking coal, manganese and nickel producer, is suffering from weak prices, pulling down its earnings. Even though the share price has fallen to reflect the weaker earnings, the PER remains high (low earnings). Back in my researcher analysis days, there was a rule that you sold resource shares on a single digit PER, as the earnings cycle was at the top, and you bought them when the PER was high, reflecting a turning point in the earning cycle. That, too, is overly simplistic, but proves the point that a low PER and high yield could be a trap of buying at the peak of earnings for a cyclical business.

Gold producers like Newcrest and energy producers like Woodside are different again. Earnings are dependent on the US-dollar–denominated gold price and oil/gas price as well as the cost of production. A low Australian dollar versus the US dollar is, generally speaking, good for all Australian resource and mining companies. This is sometimes more pronounced for gold miners if the gold price is rising as well.

Woodside is a capital-intensive business, with the costs of expansion to produce more gas often weighing on the balance sheet and potentially the dividend.

In all of these examples, there are some question marks around the sustainability of the dividend yield. As discussed in Chapter 4, cash flow management and navigating the path of expansion through increased debt are the challenges for most companies and investors.

I find gold mining shares challenging because there are too many moving parts, like the gold price, the demand for gold, the varying challenges of extracting the gold and what that does to the cost of production. Gold is often seen as a hedge against uncertainty in share markets and an easier way to play the gold theme is through a gold ETF. I explain this in more detail in Chapters 8 and 9.

Resource and gold shares can be tricky but, if you manage to pick the bottom of the cycle with the right share, it's possible to make significant capital gains in a short space of time. Timing is always important, but picking the bottom or top of cycles isn't always easy.

Second stop: banks

TABLE 5.2: The ex-growth shares – proceed with caution

Code	Company	Sector	Share price	2020 PER	2020 yield	Share price target
ANZ	ANZ	Banks	$26.61	13.0x	5.90%	$26.63
CBA	Commonwealth Bank	Banks	$90.99	18.9x	4.70%	$75.04
NAB	National Australia Bank	Banks	$27.35	13.6x	5.90%	$27.60
WBC	Westpac Banking	Banks	$25.70	14.2x	6.20%	$26.34

Source: FNArena

The banks are also often referred to as value stocks and in Australia they've been traditional favourites for share market investors. For years, bank shares were the share market darlings and great dividend payers. Then around mid-2015, the challenges and headwinds facing the banks put a dampener on the earnings party.

Macquarie, although framed as a bank, has its main business in asset management, so comparing it like-for-like with the big four – CBA, ANZ, NAB and Westpac – isn't strictly correct. It is more a diversified financial and, due to its better growth prospects, I have included it in the sleep-well-at-night shares for long-term investors.

In Table 5.2, CBA has a higher PER of around 19x and the lowest yield of the four banks at 4.7 per cent. NAB, Westpac and ANZ are all valued more cheaply at around 13-14x and have a higher dividend yield of around 6 per cent.

What is that telling us? It means that investors and the market are placing a high valuation on CBA because they think Australia's largest bank is a safer investment and offers higher quality.

All the banks have to a greater or lesser extent been through the ringer with the Royal Commission into Misconduct in the Banking, Superannuation and Financial Services Industry (commonly known as the 'Banking Royal Commission') and ongoing compliance issues. Commonwealth Bank has always been valued at a higher PER multiple of the big four, and is probably at its peak historical PER.

I used to own shares in the big banks, but now I only own Macquarie because of its earnings make-up and growth prospects; that is why I have included in it the next category of shares to own. I believe that its large, successful asset management division and the burgeoning growth in the clean energy infrastructure business is a winner. Macquarie has had its ups and downs over the years, and many investors have viewed the company as having a higher risk profile than the other four. I think Macquarie's near-death experience in the GFC resulted in a substantial rethink and orientation of the business to make Macquarie more robust and defensive. The current CEO, who grew the highly successful asset management division, has fundamentally altered the Macquarie business model for the better, I think.

The other four banks' business models are more traditional, more cyclical in terms of how the Australian economy is performing, and with a high exposure to property lending. They're very sensitive to interest rates. It's much harder for banks to make money when interest rates come down, which explains all the politics around whether the big four cut mortgage loans in line with the RBA's interest rate cuts. The more the lending margins (the difference between the rate at which a bank borrows money versus the rate at which it lends the money) are squeezed, the harder it is for banks to make money.

The banks have also continued to struggle under the weight of changing their cultures to meet the standards of the Australian Prudential Regulation Authority (APRA) and the Australian Transaction Reports and Analysis Centre (AUSTRAC), and the significant financial penalties for breaching money laundering and other financial regulations. There are concerns over the capital costs of upgrading the information technology systems in these institutions and fending off competition from disruptors and other new lending institutions. It really has been a perfect storm for the banks and that has been reflected in the cuts in dividends and flagging share prices.

In isolation, the PER and yield forecast suggest the banks are still good value, particularly the relatively lower PER and higher yield for ANZ, NAB and Westpac. But these companies are not out of the woods yet, so despite what might seem like attractive pricing and value, there's the potential for more disappointment.

Third stop: sleep-well-at-night shares

TABLE 5.3: The next nine of the top 30 for your portfolio

Code	Company	Sector	Share price	2020 PER	2020 yield	Share price target
ALL	Aristocrat Leisure	Gaming	$37.15	23.4x	1.80%	$37.29
AMC	Amcor	Packaging	$15.05	16.1x	4.60%	$16.69
ASX	Australian Stock Exchange	Financials	$82.25	31.8x	2.81%	$73.59
COL	Coles Group	Consumer Staples	$16.98	25.4x	3.30%	$15.06

Code	Company	Sector	Share price	2020 PER	2020 yield	Share price target
CSL	CSL	Health Care	$331.19	47.4x	0.90%	$326.39
MQG	Macquarie Bank	Diversified Financial	$148.58	17.3x	4.00%	$138.82
RHC	Ramsay Health Care	Health Care	$79.75	27.0x	2.00%	$70.53
WES	Wesfarmers	Conglomerate	$45.65	27.3x	3.30%	$37.37
WOW	Woolworths Group	Consumer Staples	$43.14	29.6x	2.40%	$37.44

Source: FNArena

At this bus stop, Table 5.3 shows shares from many different sectors. However, these shares all have one similar trait: they're good quality, with features that offer a more reliable and predictable earnings stream. Accordingly, you'll see the PER multiples are much higher – mostly mid-20s upwards – than those in Tables 5.1 and 5.2 – and the yields are also a lot lower, ranging from 1 to 4 per cent.

'How can this be?', you're thinking. Why would you pay so much more for a share that gives you less income? The answer lies in the detail. Aristocrat Leisure has built a highly profitable gaming business (not every investor's cup of tea on the ethical spectrum) and is successfully expanding by acquiring US digital online games. According to expert analyst research, EPS are forecast to double from 2018 to 2021, meaning earnings are growing around 30 per cent p.a. This equates to a potential 30 per cent rise in the share price for the next two years if the company achieves the analyst forecasts.

The ASX is largely a monopoly operating the Australian Securities Exchange and is also a world leading developer of the new blockchain technology that's expected to replace and disrupt the existing share settlement and custody systems. Shares in ASX have been deemed too pricey by analysts as earnings grow at a more modest pace than the likes of Aristocrat. Yet investors like me have been attracted by the yield and the reasonable reliability of earnings despite the perceived lack of value. The shares have been a good long-term performer.

Coles and Woolworths are quite straightforward. Investors have been happy to pay a higher value for the defensive and resilient nature of the earnings: we all need to go shopping! Our rising population has provided a favourable demographic backdrop in terms of more mouths to sell to. Both shares haven't been immune from some adverse publicity surrounding underpayment of staff and there's no denying that competition from Aldi and Amazon, along with Costco and other online businesses, could increase pressure on margins and profits. As the share prices show, they're moving from very fully valued to expensive, compared to the share price targets. In this instance I would exercise caution. The upcoming earnings reports will shed more light on whether the share prices are too high or the share price targets too low – that is, if the earnings forecasts are upgraded.

The global biotech superstar CSL (blood plasma, flu vaccines and gene therapies) and the popular Ramsay Health Care (private hospital operator) are on 47x and 27x PERs respectively and very low yields. CSL has been a standout share performer and is a model company for those who want to understand what makes a great business and investment. (I talk more about why CSL is such a good share investment later in this chapter, and for more in-depth analysis see the case study in the appendix.) The premium ascribed to the shares (meaning they trade on a high PER and low yield) is based on their perceived quality, reliability and growth in earnings and, I believe, the growth in dividend income over time.

Investors are happy to take growth over yield, particularly in the CSL case, as the capital gain in the share prices far outweighs a higher yield and little to no capital gain. It could be argued that some investors find CSL a more challenging company to understand, as a biotech that specialises in blood plasma, flu vaccines and the development of other speciality health drugs. This should not be an impediment to owning the shares, however. There are many expert analysts who cover the shares, with a great understanding of the businesses, and considerable online material available from respected journalists. Our job is not to be an expert analyst (how many people calculate the net interest margins for the bank shares before buying them?), but to interpret the expert opinion. Should you want to look at or listen to more information about CSL or any other company, the half-yearly and annual conference calls are an excellent starting point.

Wesfarmers is a special situation. The company is being reshaped, under the guidance of a new CEO, through assets sales like the loss-making UK Homebase business and the partial sale of Coles. The company also owns Bunnings, Officeworks, Kmart and Target, some of which are experiencing significant competitive pressure from online disruption. Investors have pushed the shares higher on the good yield and the perceived future growth from ongoing restructuring but, as the share price target shows, Wesfarmers is fully valued, based upon the current share price versus the target share price (around $46 versus around $37).

Fourth stop: infrastructure

TABLE 5.4: Favourites for income hungry investors, the next two

Code	Company	Sector	Share price	2020 PER	2020 yield	Share price target
SYD	Sydney Airport	Infrastructure	$8.58	49.6x	4.50%	$8.14
TCL	Transurban Group	Toll Roads	$16.37	80.0x	3.80%	$14.70

Source: FNArena

Now we're at the fourth bus stop, and you're probably asking yourself what's going on with the two large 'infrastructure' companies in Table 5.4? I've included the toll-road operator Transurban and the only listed airport, Sydney. Those PER multiples look crazy: sky-high at 80x and 50x respectively. Who would even think about buying a share that expensive on a PER when you could buy BHP or WBC cheaper?

The devil is in the detail for infrastructure shares. Remember how I talked about the 'lower-for-longer' era of interest rates in Chapter 3? Well, here's a prime example of investors buying into these shares because they want a safe and secure income; around 4 per cent is a good yield when cash in the bank is close to zero.

Infrastructure shares are usually valued on yield and much of the valuation is correlated to interest rates because these companies have a lot of debt which they use to build the assets, like the toll roads or renovations/expansion of the airport. The debt levels are very sensitive to what interest rates they're locked in at, so as interest rates fall, these companies can make more money due to lower funding costs. Equally, they're clever at managing the business models so that there's a balance between the future incomes generated from their assets, like the toll roads, versus the original cost of building them. As time goes on, people pay to use the toll roads and the assets become great cash cows for the business as there's a one-off construction cost.

Even with electric cars or autonomous driverless vehicles, our major cities will need toll roads. Travel and tourism should continue to benefit Sydney airport. Having said that, the tragic bushfires across NSW and Victoria, with the accompanying poor publicity across the world, and now the coronavirus, may be clouds on the horizon for Australia's tourism industry. Time will tell how this story plays out.

Share investors generally love infrastructure companies, particularly the large superannuation and pension funds that give a reasonable return on their money. However, infrastructure shares are not without risks: passenger numbers through the airport can be affected by issues such as the coronavirus, extreme weather can cause bushfires and drought, or interest rates may rise.

These share prices might be stretched in the short term, but my hunch is that any pullback in infrastructure share prices will be well supported by buyers, assuming there's no perception of interest rates rising. These shares can be sold off aggressively if there's any sniff of rising rates. A good entry point for these shares is when they go ex-distribution (dividend); that is, the cut-off day in the calendar for receiving the current dividend.

Fifth stop: property giants

TABLE 5.5: Three great real estate shares to invest in; that's 25

Code	Company	Sector	Share price	2020 PER	2020 yield	Share price target
DXS	Dexus	Real Estate	$13.18	19.8x	4.00%	$13.58
GMG	Goodman Group	Real Estate	$16.44	28.5x	1.80%	$16.46
SCG	Scentre Group	Real Estate	$3.77	15.0x	6.00%	$3.83

Source: FNArena

We Aussies love property, and why not? The returns over the decades have been lucrative for investors. So here we take a peek at the three largest property shares and I explain how different they all are. The property shares are generally called 'trusts' or real estate investment trusts (REITs) because of the structure they're held in. Depending upon the trust and management, the dividends or distributions may or may not be franked and you should check before buying if franking credits are important to you.

Starting with Scentre (see Table 5.5), these are the assets of Westfield shopping centres and malls in Australia. The PER multiple at 15x is relatively low and the dividend yield relatively high and seemingly attractive. So, what's the catch? You have to ask yourself why, if the assets were so good, did the Lowy family sell out a couple of years ago? I believe it's because online retail disruption has changed the way we all shop forever, and the trend won't disappear any time soon. Large anchor tenants of shopping malls like department stores Myer and David Jones are under pressure, and question marks remain over the long-term viability of the business model. Scentre's dividend income will be under pressure in the future as tenants try to lower or maintain the rental payments for space in the malls. Is this the type of share you want to buy or hold? Is it possibly a false economy?

Conversely, Goodman Group, which had a near-death experience in the GFC because of too much debt, has deleveraged (reduced debt) and is now an owner and developer of the large warehouses that benefit from the explosive growth in online retailing, with tenants like Amazon. Like the infrastructure shares, the Goodman share price is sensitive to rising interest rates or the perception of higher rates. However, the company is in the right space for good long-term growth.

Dexus is different again, with 60 per cent of its assets in the Sydney office space market. It has been and will probably remain a very good long-term exposure for investors. Dexus, like other property companies exposed to prime office assets, has been a significant beneficiary of offshore (overseas) companies looking to invest in prime commercial real estate in Australia's major cities.

Sixth stop: insurance/financials

TABLE 5.6: Insurance companies bringing up the rear

Code	Company	Sector	Share price	2020 PER	2020 yield	Share price target
IAG	Insurance Australia	Insurance	$6.79	21.1x	3.95%	$7.26
QBE	QBE Insurance	Insurance	$14.15	17.1x	4.80%	$14.09
SUN	Suncorp Group	Banking/Insurance	$12.57	16.3x	5.00%	$12.57

Source: FNArena

You're almost at the end of your bus journey, so hang in there for these last two stops. Insurance companies were once market darlings, but competition, natural disasters and low interest rates have made this sector challenging for shareholders.

Competition from online comparison websites like iSelect and Budget Direct will continue to challenge the businesses. The yield, 4 per cent plus, and relatively low PER multiples (mid to high teens) might seem tempting, but I haven't owned an insurance company since 2008. In the February 2020 reporting season, both IAG and SUN have downgraded earnings as a direct result of the bushfires and floods across eastern Australia. There are also future question marks over the cost of re-insurance for these companies, and higher re-insurance costs means higher insurance premiums for customers. QBE is not as exposed to the Australian natural disasters. Nevertheless, I believe that insurers are a higher risk proposition for investors.

Seventh stop: 'T' shares

TABLE 5.7: Two more – that's 30

Code	Company	Sector	Share price	2020 PER	2020 yield	Share price target
BXB	Brambles	Transportation	$12.65	22.7x	4.00%	$12.18
TLS	Telstra	Telecommunications	$3.77	19.2x	4.20%	$4.05

Source: FNArena

For lack of a better term, I have named these two shares the 'T' shares as Brambles is in transportation and logistics and Telstra, as we all know, is telecommunications. Both have good yields and reasonable-to-high PER multiples. So, what's not to like? Well, a review of their histories shows that some big household names are not necessarily the best shares.

Telstra was for many years a straight-up dividend play (a winner), with high income, until the company could no longer afford to pay out so much cash it had to cut the dividend two years in a row. The full-year dividend was halved from 31 cents in 2017 to 16 cents in 2019. It came as no surprise that the share price also halved from over $6 in 2015 to a low of $2.50 in 2018.

Telstra shareholders have been long-suffering because of a combination of competition, the NBN travails, the regulatory minefield in combination with an overzealous dividend policy, and lack of strategic investment – and now the growing competition from the Vodafone-TPG merger. The shares accordingly seem fairly valued based on the share price target and time will only tell whether the much-hyped 5G wi-fi will be the growth driver Telstra needs.

Brambles' journey has not been without hiccups. The bulk of its business is actually wooden pallets for moving freight. Its earnings and dividends, however, are on a road to nowhere – there's no growth. I don't find the 4.0 per cent yield appealing when the future is so flat.

So, there you have the ASX 30 express: seven stops and many different stories. Chapter 4 showed you the importance of the financial fundamentals, particularly the ability of shares to have sufficient cash flow to cover the debt, and this chapter exposed how it's not that straightforward! Numbers tell a multitude of tales, some good and others not so great. The expression 'oils ain't oils' comes to mind; not all oils are the same and not all shares are the same, even if the yield and PER multiples are the same.

When looking at buying or selling shares, the numerical valuation tools like the yield and the PER multiple should always be assessed within the context of the company's situation. Expressions like 'cheap for a reason' are important to keep in mind for a level-headed approach to investing.

The CSL, BHP and CBA challenge

CSL is a superstar share and its performance has blitzed that of Australia's two other largest shares, BHP and Commonwealth Bank. Although CSL has become a share market darling, it remains the least well known of the three companies and is probably the least understood.

BHP, the big Australian, is one of Australia's largest and oldest mining companies and a world leader in iron ore production.

Commonwealth Bank is a household name in Australia. It's the largest Australian bank and is perceived by investors as being of a higher quality than the other banks, but Commonwealth has experienced many problems as exposed by the recent Banking Royal Commission.

CSL was sold out of CSIRO in 1994 at an adjusted share price of $0.77 (or $2.30 at the IPO). CSL was originally created in 1916 during World War I to service the health needs of Australians who were cut off from the rest of the world. The company provided insulin, penicillin, and vaccines against the flu, polio and other dangerous diseases.

Now CSL is Australia's second-largest listed security on the ASX and is one of the world's leading biotech companies through CSL plasma, its blood plasma operations; Seqirus, the world's second-largest flu vaccine business; and Calimmune, a leader in gene modification and cell delivery technology.

If you're an existing share investor or just starting out, CSL is a good example of what's important to consider when you buy shares.

Reading the price charts

Figures 5.1, 5.2 and 5.3 show three share price charts for CSL, CBA and BHP. BHP divested (sold) its coking coal, manganese and nickel assets in May 2015 to South32, a new listed company, so I have included the South32 share price chart as well (Figure 5.4). At the time BHP shareholders received one South32 share for every BHP share and a $2.25 dividend.

The price charts show you how the shares have moved in the last ten years. You can see that only the CSL chart displays the optimal movement from the bottom left to the top right corner. The CBA and BHP charts show how cyclical prices can be and why timing for buying and selling is important.

FIGURE 5.1: CSL share price going back ten years

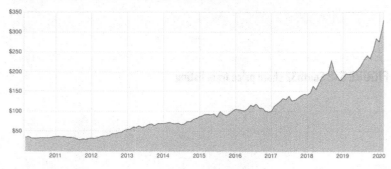

Source: Marketindex.com.au

FIGURE 5.2: CBA share price going back ten years

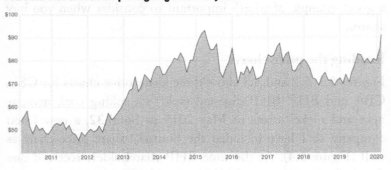

FIGURE 5.3: BHP share price going back ten years and adjusted for the sale of South32

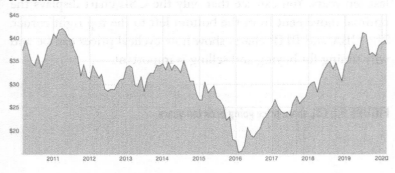

FIGURE 5.4: South32 share price from listing

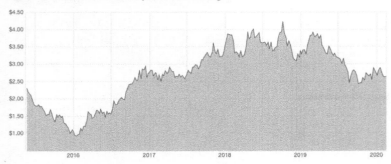

Source: Marketindex.com.au

Using the charts to show the future

To summarise what these price charts show, imagine you'd invested $1000 in CSL, CBA and BHP ten years ago and what that would look like ten years later (on 14 February 2020):

- A $1000 investment in CSL (32 shares) would be worth $10,560 and total dividend income received would be $505.41, giving a total return of $11,065.41.

- A $1000 investment in CBA (18 shares) would be worth $1620 and the total dividend income received would be $689.04, giving a total return of $2309.04.

- A $1000 investment in BHP (24 shares) would be worth $985.32 (including the 24 shares received in the South32 demerger) and the total dividend income received would be $324.55, giving a total return of $1309.87.

In comparison, if you put $1000 into the bank at an average 2 per cent p.a. you get $1200 after ten years – $109.87 less than buying 24 BHP shares!

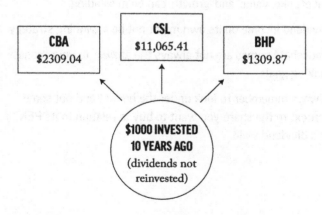

These returns are not adjusted for inflation, meaning if you account for the effect of inflation at an average of 2 per cent p.a. over the last ten years then you made no money at all putting the cash in the bank, and barely any with the BHP share purchase. Share investing allows for your savings to grow in excess of inflation, ensuring you make capital and income, not lose it. Even so, some shares, no matter how well known the name or reputation, make challenging share investments.

This example raises a lot of questions about risk. If you look at the up and downs (cycles) of the BHP share price, it's clear that timing is all-important when investing in shares. This leads to my next chapter, which focuses on emotions, bull and bear markets, share market timing and one of my favourite subjects, 21st century investing.

Chapter summary

- ► Not all shares are the same.

- ► Labels like 'value' and 'growth' can be misleading.

- ► Dividend income on its own might not be a winning strategy.

- ► Household names are not always the answer to your money-making goals.

- ► Always remember to look under the bonnet and put some context to the share you want to buy in relation to its PER and dividend yield.

6

Money, money, money: what makes the share market go round

In this chapter, I give you some insight into the idiosyncrasies of the share market. You might think this is a bit tedious but trust me, you'll thank me in time.

You've probably heard people brag about doubling their money on Afterpay (a fintech disruptor), up 149.5 per cent; a2 Milk (baby milk formula), up 46 per cent; Xero (business software), up 113 per cent; or Altium (circuit board software), up 78 per cent in 2019. Everyone likes to tell a good story about the wins, but no-one likes to tell you about the bombs, like Speedcast or RCR Tomlinson, one of Australia's oldest engineering companies that went belly up in 2019. (The appendix to this book includes case studies on some of these shares.)

I own or have owned every one of these shares. The company a2 Milk, which produces baby milk formula with the special a2 protein, made shareholders more than ten times their money in less than three years. As I said to my son at the time, 'Shares like this don't come along very often, so you need to recognise when a share is a game changer for wealth creation'.

All share investors want to own the 'tenbaggers' – shares that go up ten times. Sometimes you invest in them and get lucky, but they're not the norm. In some market conditions, it's true, it's much easier to find the tenbaggers and ride the profit gravy train. In other market conditions, though, even with the best will in the world, you'll struggle to find them and you may be left with a 'tensagger' – my word for a share price that falls indefinitely and never recovers.

What's the definition of a share price that has fallen by 90 per cent? Answer: a share price that falls 80 per cent and halves again.

Honest investors will reveal that they have a store of tensaggers stuffed in the proverbial share bottom drawer. Yet they're forever hopeful that the shares will eventually recover to the purchase price. Remember that hot tip that couldn't go wrong, and lo and behold it did? It's never too late to sell.

The investors who make millions and survive the turbulence of share market cycles are just as adept at dodging the losers as picking the winners. You can't kiss all the beautiful girls or boys!

This chapter reveals how to identify the type of market you're trading in, how the world of investing is changing in the 21st century, and what matters most so you can be part of the money-making trends. Let's start with the different types of share markets and how that makes a difference to share investing.

Keeping your emotions in check

All markets are made up of humans buying and selling assets, like shares. Sure, there are computer-generated share-trading models, referred to as algorithms, but humans write the models and many remain active participants, and we're all emotional creatures. Even expert investors will have fallen prey to emotions at some stage in their investment career.

What do emotions have to do with shares? If you've never bought a share and seen the share price double or halve, it's extremely difficult to understand or appreciate how a moving share price can impact on your psyche. When you personally invest 'your' money, not someone else's money, movements in the share prices give you real and visceral feelings. It's a bit like your first love or your first real break-up! One makes you blissfully euphoric and the other breaks your heart.

Rising share prices make you feel excited because you can see your riches growing. Falling shares prices make you feel horrid, even depressed. Remember the sad tales of traders committing suicide after the 1929 Wall Street crash?

To be a good and resilient investor, you need to understand how your emotions and the collective emotions feed into share markets and move share prices, sometimes to extreme highs or lows.

Greed and the desire for more profits create 'FOMO' – fear of missing out. This is the emotion that makes share investors buy a share because everyone else is buying it and it's going up. This can result in a bubble-like scenario. As shown in the table in Chapter 4, bubbles are at the extreme end of the valuation spectrum when prices are being driven by everything except logic and reason.

Fear of not being able to stop losing money is termed 'FONGO' – fear of not getting out. When everyone else starts selling a share, panic can set in and we all want to stop the pain of seeing our profits or money disappear or the bubble possibly bursting.

A popular expression in the industry is 'share prices take the stairs up and the elevator down'. This means that share prices go up gradually, but they can crash quickly when going down in value. It's hard to convince someone to buy a new share, so investors move more slowly into the market than when there's bad news or big sell-off. Humans are programmed to avoid loss, ahead of awaiting long-term profit. We tend to have a herd-like mentality, and sometimes act irrationally to be part of the gang. We all tend to jump on board a trend eventually.

The feelings of greed and fear are very much related to timing how you invest in the share market. Like many things in life, timing is everything. There are some shares, like CSL, which, if you bought at any time since they listed on the stock exchange and held, you would have made money.

In contrast, BHP is cyclical, and making money in that share depends on at what point in the cycle you buy and sell. If you bought BHP in 2011, the share price was around $45; it then fell to $14.50 in late 2015 before rising to $41 in mid-2019. So, with a commodity-related share like BHP or any of the resource companies, timing is crucial. If you bought and held from 2011, as the example in Chapter 5 showed, it would've barely returned more than inflation, meaning your investment was not working.

If you'd bought any of the four superstars like Afterpay, a2 Milk, Altium or Xero in the last two years, it would've been prudent to take some profits along the way.

You can't go wrong taking a profit or some profit, but you can go wrong not selling when the wheels start to fall off. To make a good decision, and manage your greed and fear, you need to return to looking at the fundamentals and remember that analysing the numbers like the PER and yield only gets you so far. Remember, also, to look under the bonnet and see if the share is trading in a particular part of the cycle.

In Chapter 9 I give you a guide as to what rules to use and show you how to put together a portfolio of shares.

Happy as a bull, grumpy as a bear

In periods when everything is rosy for shares – profits are rising, dividends are flowing in or interest rates are falling and shares are being supported by the RBA's liquidity (refer to Chapter 3) – then most share prices go up. This is often referred to as a 'bull' market. The year 2019 was a good bull market but 2020 (at time of writing) is extremely volatile as the grey clouds of concern gather around the impact of coronavirus on growth. The longer the virus spreads, the greater the impact on world growth, earnings and share prices. Just about anyone could have made money in the Australian share market if they bought in late 2018 or the beginning of January 2019.

Of course, some shares made investors poorer like Speedcast, but the ASX 200 index is up a very nice 19 per cent excluding dividends, or 24 per cent including dividends. So if you had just bought the index at the end of 2018, you could have turned $1000 into $1240; or $10,000 into $12,400.

Conversely, if you look back at 2018, the picture was not so nice. The ASX 200 took share investors on a roller-coaster ride throughout the year and eventually ended down 7.7 per cent. If you added back dividends it would have resulted in around only a 3.7 per cent fall in value for the market. It was hard to find many shares that went up in the last quarter of 2018, so doubling your money would have been impossible.

Bull markets like 2019 make investors feel great and usually most people, new or experienced, can make money.

Following the trends

You may hear the terms 'momentum investing' or 'trend following'. Some share traders/investors purely follow the trends or the upward or downward momentum of a share price using various trading models. They pick the shares going up and they buy them. Conversely, they pick the shares going down and sell them.

Like most models, these can work some of the time but not all of the time, otherwise everyone would use the method and making money would be easy. However, you need to keep in the back of your mind that the trend is usually your friend and timing when you buy and sell is important. More about this in Chapter 9 where I describe a charting method known as Dow theory.

Bear markets, when share prices fall, are extremely challenging for any investor, and that's when dividends matter. Not all bull markets turn into bubbles when, for any number of reasons, irrational exuberance takes hold and pushes share prices to ridiculous levels, sometimes resulting in share market crashes like those of 1929, 1987, 2001 and 2008. Most bull markets don't end in a crash, however, so not all bear markets are as severe as these five. In these cases, it was usually a specific event that led to the crash – in 2008 it was excessive lending and the subprime loans in the USA. If you are seeking more information and understanding, look no further than the book *The Big Short* by Michael Lewis or the film of the same name.

In bull markets liquidity, or the ability to buy and sell shares, is normally high and investors can buy and sell fairly easily – without having to move the share price too much. In bear markets liquidity is thin and light; no-one is really buying shares, so if you want to sell it can be hard to transact without the share prices falling a lot. Share market volumes and the value of shares traded are usually characteristically high in bull market times, but low in bear markets.

It may sound like a no-brainer to some readers, but shares don't just trade by themselves – there has to be a real buyer and seller on either side of the trade. Only 30 years ago you could go to the stock exchange and see real people buying and selling shares on sliding chalk boards! Now all trades are conducted electronically. I once heard a story about an investor who rang his stockbroker and said, 'I want to buy $1000 of ABC company'. The next day he looked in the paper and saw the price of ABC had gone up. He thought, 'Great!', and he rang his stockbroker and said, 'Buy $1000 more!' This went on for a few days until the share price had risen 50 per cent and he thought it time to take his profits. He rang his stockbroker and told him to sell and his stockbroker said, 'That might be a problem'. 'Why?' he enquired. 'Well', said the stockbroker, 'the thing is, you were the only buyer and as the only buyer, you pushed the share price up!'

Boom! Big lesson: liquidity, particularly in 'small cap' shares (small companies), is incredibly important. In bull markets the small caps can double merely by having too many buyers and momentum. However, when the music stops or the truth about the company is revealed there's not enough liquidity to sell and those great tenbagger tips become the tensaggers.

Bull markets are a boon for sellers and bear markets are a boon for the brave buyers.

Normally what happens is at the top of a bull market, everyone is buying, creating a euphoric top in the share market, sometimes a bubble. The converse is true for the low of a bear market, when no-one wants shares and no-one is buying or selling.

Here's some good news: I don't believe we have reached a euphoric top of a bull market at the time of writing in early February 2020 (although it's looking fully priced in the short term). As long as we have a lower-for-longer interest rate environment, there will always be good share buying opportunities, so waiting for a pull-back or a sell-off in the market is prudent.

Bear markets don't have to happen. Bear markets come about because earnings are falling and economies are slowing, or if there's some nasty shock from a hike in interest rates, for example, to arrest a spike in inflation.

The experts usually tell us that bull and bear markets have very specific characteristics, but for our purposes I don't think it's important to dwell on those. Here's all you need to know:

► Almost anyone can make money in bull markets.

► Transaction volumes are usually higher in bull markets.

► Bull markets usually last longer than bear markets.

► Everyone can lose interest in a bear market but there's money to be made in such a market, just not 'easy money'.

► Sustainable dividends matter in both bull and bear markets but more so in bear markets when share prices fall or flatline (I explain the importance of dividends in full in Chapter 7).

Twenty-first century investing

Have you started to understand that some of the share market stalwarts and mainstays, like BHP and CBA, haven't been the best money-makers for investors? The truth is that the times are changing. I'm going to stick my head out and say, as we move into the third decade of the 21st century, 'it's different this time'.

In this section, in the interests of taking a simple but thorough approach to share investing and fundamentals, I talk about how the 21st century businesses that have emerged in the technological, biomedical, internet and data innovations era have created debate among research analysts and experts. Money will continue to be made and lost as new businesses and technologies emerge and old businesses struggle to adapt and change. Share investors need to be open-minded about our changing world. It's the start of a new decade and there's no better time to reset and calibrate the way we think about investing. As Mark Twain reportedly said, 'History never repeats itself but it often rhymes'.

In the USA, Netflix has been named the top-performing share in the S&P 500 index for the last decade, up over 4000 per cent. To put that into perspective, $1000 invested is now worth $41,000 in US dollar terms. Netflix has disrupted the entire TV and entertainment industry through the development of streaming, enabled by improved internet speeds (this varies across countries and Australia) and an incredible amount of money spent on creating bingeable content. The company also challenges every element of fundamental analysis (eye-watering levels of debt, razor-thin margins and loss making), which makes the shares even more difficult to understand.

The acceleration of technological and digital change that started in the late 1990s with the evolution of the internet has now become a firmly entrenched feature of some of the world's largest companies.

Some commentators have compared the emergence of the tech-nology behemoths (think Facebook, Amazon, Google, Netflix and Apple in the USA) to the equivalent of the size and extent of change created in the development of the railways across America in the 19th century. This gives you some indication of the impact and wealth creation these companies have had, partic-ularly in the past decade. Correspondingly, these companies have brought with them some significant challenges to the investment community, including how to analyse and value the companies.

How can you value a company that doesn't have a traditional business model and fixed assets like a car manufacturer, an iron ore producer or a brick maker? How can software-as-a-service (SaaS) be valued if the company only has intellectual property or human intellect; that is, people who work as coders and programmers and a business based in the cloud?

For most of us it's just too abstract to understand, unless of course you're like my son who is studying mechatronic engineering (coding and artficial intelligence – AI) at university. It took me a while to understand that the 'cloud' isn't a bubble in the sky where information and data goes, but the term for software systems and banks of computers stored in specially constructed buildings.

Tech behemoths like Amazon, Microsoft and Google are leading world businesses in cloud-based software systems. Valuing these technology companies has and continues to be a very hotly debated issue in the share investment world and isn't going away any time soon.

Many of these 21st century businesses – like Netflix, Amazon, Google, Salesforce and Atlassian in America and Xero, Wisetech, Appen and Technology One in Australia – are measured to some degree on a price to revenue basis, instead of a PER ratio. Many of these companies spend so much capital investing for the future that they choose not to turn a profit (inasmuch as they can). It's by no means the first time in history that businesses have invested heavily in infrastructure to grow their operations for the future. The problem some investors have is that the infrastructure isn't visible; it's not a railway, a mine with a producible resource, a factory or a shop. The resources are banks of people sitting at computers doing whatever it is they do, which most of us don't understand. How do you value people?

The tag 'growth' is typically applied to these companies and the investment world is divided on the valuations placed on the shares. As an investor, you need to understand that these businesses are very different to the traditional steel makers, manufacturing or energy companies of the 20th century, but they can and do offer excellent money-making opportunities.

Part of the concern is that our low-interest-rate world has artificially supported the creation of these technology businesses (through large amounts of debt) and boosted the valuations. Many experts firmly believe that these businesses would not survive if interest rates went up and many refer to the dotcom crash to illustrate what can befall technology shares. I beg to differ! Most of these businesses are massive cash flow generators and could generate a profit if management chose to not invest so much (although growth rates would slow and that would put pressure on the valuation). Also, I see no evidence that interest rates will return to even pre-GFC levels any time soon.

The value of intellectual property

Here's a story to explain the intangible asset of human intellect. It occurred back in the 1990s when I worked in London. It was early 1995 and my then employer of five years, Barings Securities, went bust, thanks to some avarice and reckless trading. At the time, I was in Indonesia with a client who worked for one of the world's largest emerging markets' investment companies (these are the active fund managers who invest in emerging markets on behalf of their clients – people like us or institutional money like super funds). Thankfully, when we returned to London and the dust settled, the Dutch group ING Bank kindly put their hand up to buy Barings Bank for £1 and £800 million of debt.

Apparently, the ING representative mistakenly told the staff on the trading room floor of Barings Securities that he was very happy ING had bought Barclays! Not only had ING bought Barings not Barclays, the company also received a rude shock when Barings' management informed ING that it owed the staff bonuses a few months later.

Having just spent £800 million and £1, the thought of a few more million in bonuses for a business that had gone under didn't sit too well with ING management. However, it was pointed out to them that if they did not guarantee the Barings staff their bonuses and a guaranteed bonus for the next 12 months then they had, in fact, bought nothing but some office leases, office furniture and computers. The new owners capitulated.

The point is that Barings' value lay in its name and staff. We weren't hard or fixed assets but intellectual property – human capital (in theory) and reputation. So poor ING had to fork out a lot more money to keep the Barings business going.

Technology and innovation are here to stay. Whether we like it or not, we're in a new era of investing that involves data, AI in varying forms, space tourism, electric vehicles, autonomous driverless vehicles, 5G wireless technology, the internet-of-things smart houses, gene therapies, biotechnology and alternative meat products. It's a bit like the boiling frog syndrome: sometimes we're living it so much we don't see the change.

I profess to be an early adopter when it comes to share investing. I love reading about the new companies and their technologies or disruptive innovations, whether it's Richard Branson's Virgin Galactic (the world's first rocket for space tourism) or Elon Musk's transformation of the car manufacturing and energy industries, Tesla. I invest directly into US shares so that I'm in tune with what's occurring in other share markets. Yet some of these new trends can push the share prices very high, very quickly, so when investing in new technology shares exercise caution as 'blue sky' euphoria (hope and expectation) can overtake what is actually realistic in terms of the company's financials.

It's hard for us in Australia to appreciate the level of change happening in the USA and the rest of the world. Australians are highly educated and great innovators. Three of our premier health care, biotech and biomedical companies are world leaders: CSL, Resmed (sleep apnoea solutions) and Cochlear (hearing implants). Yet, technology companies are not as well captured in the Australian share market.

However, the tide is turning and the ASX has recently announced the intention to create a technology index, like the Nasdaq. The ASX is actively supporting technology companies domestically and from around the world to list in Australia. One day, hopefully, the tech giants like Atlassian will not have to go to America to list on Nasdaq but will have a suitable support network and platform in Australia.

Risks for shares in the next decade

In this section, as the first year of the 2020s unfolds, it's worthwhile pausing to think about what risks could erode the performance of shares and what investment themes you should keep an eye out for. I think the one forecast I can make confidently is that risk will be the word that sums up the next decade for investors.

Disruption

Don't underestimate how much many forms of disruption will challenge businesses old and new, be they technological, ideological or regulatory. We're living in a period of massive change and the best businesses and share investments will be attuned to not only the change but also the mood of the customers, shareholders and general public. There's no better example than what has happened with the Australian banks as a result of the Banking Royal Commission and the ongoing regulatory pressures.

Business as usual, where the shareholders are the sole beneficiaries, is no longer acceptable and many businesses will require what's termed as a 'social licence' to operate; it's not about just making money. Other stakeholders like the customers, the employees and the environment, for example, will matter. In 2019, some of the best-performing shares like CSL and Altium deliberately disrupted their own products and services in order to maintain a competitive advantage. They're the type of shares you want to own – shares of companies whose management is wholly in tune with all the moving parts of generating a profit and return for shareholders.

Climate change

The Australian 2019/2020 summer could be a pivotal time of realisation that there are real costs and risks for businesses from climate change. The extreme weather, including higher temperatures, lower rainfall, bushfires and flooding rains, has implications for the Australian economy and many businesses and shares. Some areas and industries that will be affected are tourism (Sydney Airport and airlines like Qantas and Virgin); infrastructure (electricity producers like AGL and Origin); food retailers like Woolworths and Coles; wine producers like Treasury Wines; insurance companies; coal and gas companies (New Hope, Whitehaven, Woodside); resource giants BHP, Rio and Fortescue; and, over time, developers and engineering companies. Not only will shareholders want to see company management take the issue of climate change seriously, they will also want to know what the costs and the risks are for the shares, including the risks of what are termed 'stranded assets'. These are assets that become less valuable or worthless due to climate change or carbon abatement advances.

The political optics around the issue of climate change in Australia belies what's actually happening in the investment area overseas, including in the USA and Europe. One of the most notable recent examples is when the CEO of the world's largest fund manager, BlackRock which has US$6 trillion of assets under management, announced that climate change was now an economic and financial threat and that BlackRock has committed to selling fossil fuel investments such as coal from the actively managed funds.

A well-known American share commentator, CNBC's Jim Cramer, caused a stir at the end of January 2020 when he said on live TV, 'I'm done with fossil fuels'. Whereupon he went on to explain that fossil fuel shares are the new tobacco companies and large pension funds in the USA and Europe are shunning them due to climate change risks and a changing focus from younger investors. He didn't say fossil fuels like oil would disappear overnight; rather that they are no longer good share investments.

The converse can be seen in how companies investing in new technologies for clean energy (zero carbon emissions) are performing very strongly, such as Macquarie Bank, Tesla and NextEra Energy in the USA. How do I know? I own all of these shares. The fact that they are part of the new world paradigm of reducing emissions and the growing demand for their products and services makes them attractive to investors.

Populism – politics as determined by ordinary people

Examples of populism are Brexit and the US–China trade war. Politics is reshaping the way business is being done and global trade is transacted. One of the many reasons for the rise in populism is the increasing divergence between the rich and the poor. Shareholders have protested against excess salaries and sky-high bonuses, seeking to redress the power imbalances.

Ethics and governance

The younger generation, in particular, is influencing how businesses operate and, as a result, share prices. Alternative meat products with a lower carbon footprint, companies that manage climate risk and businesses that don't use slave labour are just a few examples of how investment trends will change and evolve in the next decade. The steep increase in sustainable and ESG investment products and funds under management is indicative of this ongoing trend in investing for 'good'.

Share investment opportunities for the 2020s

➤ Australia's top health care and biotech shares CSL, Resmed and Cochlear. The outlook for health care this decade and beyond remains well supported by global demographics. Like any share, nothing should be taken for granted, but this sector remains one of my favourites. I explain in more detail why in the next chapter.

➤ High-quality technology companies with good products and services. There are a few in this category in Australia including Altium, Xero, Technology One and REA. There will also be new names entering this space, so keep an eye on the areas of technology.

- Infrastructure shares like Transurban, Atlas Arteria, Auckland International and possibly Sydney Airport should be good shares, assuming there's no dramatic rise in interest rates.

- Good-quality property players like Goodman Group and Charter Hall have the potential to continue to feed into the long-term secular trends of internet retail (industrial), high quality commercial and social infrastructure assets and income.

The Australian banks, I believe, remain fundamentally challenged, as I explained in Chapter 5. This means they are definitely not my preferred buys, as there are too many potential problems, including increased competition from the likes of neobanks (new low-cost online banking systems), the increased risk of capital raising to meet regulatory capital ratios; the costs of upgrading their computer systems and lower interest rates for longer. My personal preference, as I mentioned in Chapter 5, is for Macquarie Bank, which has a more diversified earnings composition and exposure to clean energy assets.

I talk about more technology and investment themes in Chapter 9 and how you can use ETF products to gain exposure to shares in these sectors overseas.

A word of caution when investing in new technology companies or new trends: be mindful of fads and bubbles. As has always been the case, share bubbles can emerge in any newly hyped investment areas. Recent bubbles include lithium and cannabis shares, streaming companies and alternative meat producers. This is how markets work. A company invests in a business where there's an opportunity. As the business grows it attracts more competitors and only the fittest survive. Sometimes it's best to sit out the early investment phase and see which shares survive and become the market leader.

All of this leads to my next chapter, where I discuss everything you need to know about what makes a great share investment: identifying quality shares, the importance of dividends and how your share investments can be future proofed. Then in Chapter 8 I show you how to navigate the world of indirect investing (managed funds and ETFs).

Chapter summary

- ► Be mindful of your emotions when you're share investing.

- ► Know about the impacts of the bull and the bear market.

- ► Anyone can make money in a bull market.

- ► Bear markets are challenging and characterised by low volumes.

- ► Fear and greed can undermine your investment decisions; stick to a plan and do your research.

- ► The 21st century will be defined by risk but opportunities will exist; be open to new ideas.

- ► It really is different this time!

7

Dividend champions and the all-stars

Shareplicity is all about how to make money in the share market in such a way that you can sleep well at night and build resilient groups of shares that can generate income and create wealth. It's not a book about how to be a day trader or trade your way to wealth. Most of us have neither the time nor energy to give up our day job to trade shares, and even if we did there would be no guarantees we would make it.

As author and former hedge fund manager Jim Cramer said on Twitter recently, 'Day trading is extremely difficult and requires a level of knowledge and discipline that few have or can attain'.

At the heart of this chapter is the fact that not all 'blue chip' shares that pay high dividends are the best share investments. A set-and-forget approach to share investing, and assuming history will repeat itself, is not the way to go when you're setting up your investment portfolio.

So, if the blue chips are not necessarily the best money-making ideas, then what are? In this chapter, I clue you in on better ways to make money and give you some examples. To achieve your goals you need to focus on shares that meet a set of criteria. I call them the 'dividend champions' and the 'all-stars'.

The grapevine and the vigneron

Remember the analogy of the vigneron and the grapevine back in Chapter 4, where I explained the difference between EPS and DPS? The growth in the vine stalks and the stems are the EPS and the grapes yielded are the DPS. I want to go back to that again because many investors fail to understand the principle and continue to buy the wrong shares.

Let's say you invest $10,000 in a number of grapevines and a vineyard. In the first year, your vineyard produces grapes worth $1000. You decide that you'll use $500 to reinvest back in the grapevines to ensure more stems and stalks grow and more grapes are produced the next year. You pay yourself $400. The remaining $100 is popped into the bank to build some cash savings for the business in case there's an unforeseen event such as a heavy frost that ruins one of the vines and you need to replace it.

In the second year, the grapevine has grown more and produces 20 per cent more than the first year, or $1200. You do the same thing: you reinvest half to expand the grapevines ($600); you pay yourself 80 per cent of the balance ($480), and you put the remaining $120 in the bank. Thereafter the vines produce 10 per cent more revenue in grapes each year and you follow the same process of reinvesting half of the value of the revenue from the grapes, paying yourself 80 per cent of the balance as a dividend and banking the rest. This same process is repeated for ten years. After ten years, this is what your grapevine business would look like.

TABLE 7.1: Option 1 - the vineyard over ten years with reinvestment

Years	Total revenue ($)	Reinvestment ($)	Dividend ($)	Deposit ($)
One	1000	500	400	100
Two	1200	600	480	120
Three	1320	660	528	132
Four	1452	726	581	145
Five	1597	799	639	160
Six	1757	879	703	176
Seven	1932	966	773	193
Eight	2126	1063	850	213
Nine	2338	1169	935	234
Ten	2572	1286	1029	257
Total	17,294	8648	6918	1730

Your $10,000 initial grapevine investment has successfully grown the revenue income from grapes sold to $2752 in the tenth year. The dividend you pay yourself has increased from $400 to $1029 in the tenth year (the yield has increased from 4 per cent to 10.26 per cent), and the total dividend income is $6918.

At the outset the vineyard was valued on a PER of 10x, the cost was $10,000 and it made you $1000 in the first year. If you now decided to sell after ten years, and applied a PER of 10x, the business would be worth $25,720. Including the dividend income of $6918, you have more than tripled your initial investment to $32,638.

In reality, the business would probably be worth more than 10x, as you have $1730 cash in the bank.

Here's another scenario (shown in Table 7.2): let's say you were a bit greedier and wanted the $1000 from the first year all for yourself and didn't reinvest any of the revenue income over the ten years. At best you could hope that the vineyard manages to produce annual revenue of $1000 p.a. but, in reality, the yield would most likely fall with no funds invested. I'm not sure about your green thumb, but I know that my plants need nutrients, water and my labour to sustain them, and that costs money and time.

With no cash in the bank and a depleted vine after ten years of no investment, I think it's safe to assume you may not even receive your initial capital of $10,000 back if you tried to sell. So you may have extracted a higher annual income, at best $1000 p.a., but a lower sale price of $9400 and a highly optimistic total income of $9400. If you can sell the vineyard you might receive $18,800. Compare this to the minimum of $32,638 in Table 7.1!

TABLE 7.2: Option 2 – the vineyard over ten years with no reinvestment

Years	Total revenue ($)	Reinvestment ($)	Dividend ($)	Deposit ($)
One	1000	0	1000	0
Two	1000	0	1000	0
Three	1000	0	1000	0
Four	1000	0	1000	0
Five	1000	0	1000	0
Six	1000	0	1000	0
Seven	1000	0	1000	0
Eight	900	0	900	0
Nine	800	0	800	0
Ten	700	0	700	0
Total	9400	0	9400	0

Option 2 reflects how you have swapped capital growth for short-term income. The vines would have withered and shrunk with no investment, meaning the value could fall to zero and you could end up with nothing.

So how does this translate back into the world of shares? Very simply, the vineyard example in option 1 is exactly the type of share you want to own. You want to own shares in businesses that grow the revenue and reinvest for the future as well as growing the dividend and putting cash away for a rainy day.

You don't want to buy or hold shares that pay high dividends at the expense of the long-term future growth of the business.

Franking credits and the imputation system

Let's put the vineyard example into practice in the Australian share market. You start by observing how companies pay dividends and determine what the yield is: it's the annual DPS divided by the share price. You then find out the payout ratio: this is the number that shows what percentage of profits the company pays out in dividends. In the vineyard example it's the dividend divided by the income: in option 1, it was 40 per cent and in option 2, it was 100 per cent.

In Australia, our dividends are unusual because of what's known as franking credits. In 1987, the government introduced the imputation system, which was designed to stop the tax office from 'double dipping'. Pre-1987, a company would pay out a dividend from its after-tax earnings (profits). The shareholder would then pay tax on the dividend income at the marginal rate.

The imputation system was designed to allow companies to pass on a tax credit to the shareholder for the percentage of tax paid on their profits, known as a franking credit. The more tax paid in Australia, the higher the franking credit for the shareholder. Here's an example to illustrate how this works:

- Company A pays a full rate of tax at 30 per cent. If it makes $100 per share and pays you $70 after tax, it means you receive a dividend of $70 and a franking tax credit of $30.

- If you pay tax at a marginal rate of 20 per cent, that means you pay $20 on the $100 dividend, but as the company has already paid $30 you receive the $10 difference.

- If you pay tax at a 40 per cent rate, you owe $40 on the dividend but as the company has already paid $30 you only need to pay the tax department $10 – this is the difference between what the company paid and you paid.

Franking credits have had a substantial effect on the Australian share market. Since the imputation system's introduction in 1987, according to data compiled by the RBA, the payout ratio in Australia has diverged from the US market. The Australian average payout has gone from around 60 per cent to over 80 per cent at times. The only period when the US market payout ratio was comparable to Australia's was during 2008 when company earnings fell but boards maintained the dividend (lower earnings and static dividends from the previous period increases the payout ratio).

The trend can be seen in an RBA discussion paper by Thomas Mathews called *A History of Australian Equities*, and most likely reflects that banks, financials and resource companies represent a large proportion of the Australian shares listed. The high payout also reflects how these companies have taken the strategic decision to continue to pay high dividends to shareholders. The problem lies in the fact that this policy works well when earnings are growing, but when the earnings slow or come under pressure the dividend can be cut. Those of you who own bank shares (with the exception of CBA) would be all too aware of the cut in dividends.

TABLE 7.3: Dividends in cents per share for the banks

Bank	2013	2014	2015	2016	2017	2018	2019
ANZ	164	178	181	160	160	160	160
CBA	364	401	420	420	421	431	431
NAB	190	198	198	198	198	198	166
WBC	194	182	187	188	188	188	174
SUN	85	108	80	71	77	74	52
BOQ	58	66	74	76	84	76	65

Source: Marketindex.com.au

Table 7.3 depicts how every bank excluding CBA cut the dividend at some point. Companies can be forced to cut the payout to shareholders when earnings are under pressure, which is not good news for shareholders!

The share price charts in Figures 7.1 to 7.4 show very clearly the negative impacts of cutting the dividends on the share price.

FIGURE 7.1: Share price chart for Commonwealth Bank going back ten years

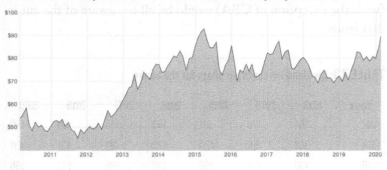

FIGURE 7.2: Share price chart for Westpac going back ten years

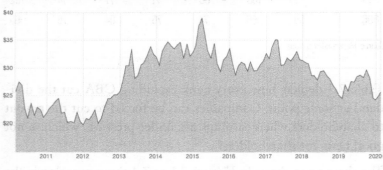

FIGURE 7.3: Share price chart for National Australia Bank going back ten years

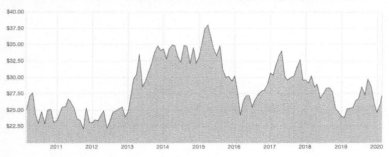

Source: Marketindex.com.au

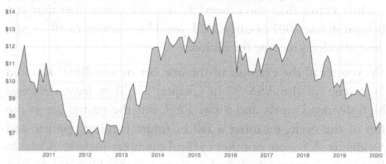

FIGURE 7.4: Share price chart for Bank of Queensland going back ten years

Source: Marketindex.com.au

Shares that pay high dividends are not necessarily the best

Figures 7.1 to 7.4 are not pretty pictures for share investors. The share prices in 2020 are below the levels achieved in 2015, meaning that if you bought bank shares in May 2015 around the top, your capital would have been reduced, in some instances by as much as 34 per cent (in the case of NAB). If that isn't sobering enough then spare a thought for some long-term shareholders – the NAB share price is still 40 per cent below the late 2007 high of just over $41.

If you go back to the vineyard example, high dividends and yield and a high payout ratio are not always good investments. High dividends can often mean one of three things:

1. a falling share price

2. a poor outlook for future earnings

3. a one-off special dividend.

Yes, bank shares are good investments that you can own or buy for the dividend income, but be aware that the banks have been capital killers (with the exception of CBA, which is tracking slightly better than the others). If you sell shares now that you bought in late 2007 or early 2015, you'd lose money. In effect, you swap dividend income for capital.

Do you recall the example of the iron ore miners BHP, Rio and Fortescue (in the ASX 30 in Chapter 5)? They have attractive high dividend yields and a low PER, but the profits are at the top of the cycle, meaning a fall in future earnings, profits and dividends. A couple of other cyclical examples include Adelaide Brighton Cement, which had an unsustainably high payout and is forecast to cut its dividend 75 per cent in its 2019 result, and Nufarm, which paid no dividend in 2019.

Bank shares, with their juicy high yields and tempting franking credit (as they pay a full rate of tax), are irresistible to some investors. However, like the option 2 vineyard scenario, they have been more intent on paying large dividends to shareholders than investing in the businesses. The banks have problems with their information technology systems and infrastructure that will necessitate a good degree of capital expenditure in the next couple of years, so returns from these shares could remain under pressure. There are also some question marks around the strength of their capital ratios, possibly resulting in further equity raisings.

All this means you need to select your shares carefully. Shares that pay high dividends may be a false economy; the dividend may decrease in the future and the share price may fall. These examples should also cause you to question the theory of 'buy and hold and she'll be right'. Buying cyclical businesses can be very tricky in terms of making money!

Blue chips aren't always the best

The large Australian shares like the banks and the mining companies are often referred to as 'blue chips' – the perception is that they can do no wrong and are as safe as houses. I hope that the analysis provided in *Shareplicity* suggests this narrative might not be true. It takes a long time to shift perceptions, and while the banks and resource shares are not going to disappear, they may not be the best option either.

Blue chips can turn into what I call 'death stars'. Look no further than AMP. Listed in January 1998, the shares traded as high as $21 in 1999 when NAB launched an unsuccessful takeover bid. Although the Janus Henderson business has since been demerged (in conjunction with a billion-dollar rights issue), the shares are now trading at $1.89, 21 years later. In 2019 the dividend was more than halved from $0.29 to $0.14. The travails of AMP have been well documented and it remains to be seen if the new CEO can revive the business. This is a classic example of a blue chip's fall from grace.

I have heard of someone who reinvested all the AMP dividends back into the shares and on retirement was shocked to see that their nest egg had actually shrunk, in spite of all the income.

The fact is that not all blue chips will stay as the best share investments. As John Paul Getty reportedly said, 'In times of rapid change experience could be your own worst enemy'.

Defining a champion share: dividends don't lie

Going back to option 1 in your vineyard, you want to buy shares that can grow the revenue, invest for the future, grow net profit and grow your dividends, while operating in a competitive and changing world.

What's the one characteristic that you want from your shares? The answer is a company that has a quality known as a strong 'moat', or competitive advantage, and potentially high barriers to entry. These are features that make a company more resilient and different from the competition. It can manifest in many ways, such as a low cost of production (BHP and Rio iron ore); customer loyalty and strong branding (Apple and Microsoft); robust intellectual property and innovation (CSL, Resmed and Cochlear); and quality assets with great locations (high quality property companies like Charter Hall and Goodman Group). Some investors would include monopolies like Sydney Airport and Transurban that have a strong grip on the business with no real competition.

In Table 7.4 I give you a selection of shares that might fit the bill for the option 1 vineyard case. I include a mixture from different industries and sectors over the last six years – these are my champion shares.

TABLE 7.4: Dividends in cents from the 'champions' over the last six years

Company	2013	2014	2015	2016	2017	2018	2019
TNE	5.60	8.16	8.78	9.45	9.96	10.46	11.90
ALL	14.50	16.00	17.00	25.00	34.00	46.00	56.00
CSL	102.00	113.00	124.00	126.00	136.00	172.00	185.00
RMD	6.20	10.90	15.80	16.80	17.40	19.20	21.40
TCL	32.50	37.50	42.50	48.00	54.50	57.00	61.00
MQG	225.00	290.00	360.00	450.00	485.00	535.00	610.00
GMG	20.50	21.45	23.00	24.98	29.65	29.25	30.00
ALU	11.00	12.00	16.00	20.00	23.00	27.00	34.00
COH	252.00	254.00	190.00	230.00	270.00	300.00	330.00
AMC	36.70	42.90	52.96	55.35	55.45	58.82	81.00

Company	2013	2014	2015	2016	2017	2018	2019
REA	41.50	57.00	70.00	81.50	91.00	109.00	118.00
CAR	28.30	32.10	35.30	37.30	1.50	44.20	45.50

Source: Marketindex.com.au; carsales.com.au; rea-group.com; CSL.com

Note: CSL dividends were declared in US dollars but paid to shareholders in Australian dollars.

To determine whether a share has been a good investment you need look no further than the historical dividends. Dividends are a cash payment, so no matter how much a company may use some accounting magic on the financial statements, the one aspect that cannot be fiddled is the cash payout dividend.

If you were to look at any of the share price charts of these companies you would see you could have made great capital returns over this period. For example, Altium (ALU) has risen from around $1.25 to almost $36; Technology One (TNE) from around $1.40 to $8.80; Aristocrat (ALL) from $3.20 to $34.60; Resmed (RMD) from $4.42 to $22.40; REA from $18 to $108; and Macquarie Group (MQG) from $34 to almost $140.

You'll make the most money by buying shares that grow earnings and dividends. Most of the shares mentioned haven't traded on a high yield; however, if you bought Altium at $1.24 the yield would be 27 per cent. Aristocrat at $3.19 would yield almost 18 per cent in 2019; even CSL would yield over 5 per cent.

Shares cannot generate the shareholder a greater return in dividends if the company isn't making more money. It's as simple as that. Too many of us fall for the trap of a high yielding share, only to be disappointed.

The fact that most of the shares in the dividend champions trade on a higher PER is reflective of the fact that investors want to buy and own shares that will make them both a capital and income gain in a low-growth, low-interest-rate world.

Reporting time is 'confession season' for companies. As highlighted in Chapter 4, companies report half-year and full-year earnings, some above and some below the market's expectations. The dividend champions are not immune from disappointment, and in times of great uncertainty – such as the February 2020 reporting season, with the impact of the coronavirus – share prices can be very volatile (move up and down a lot). In these periods, good-quality dividend payers may be sold off due to short-term or medium-term impacts, meaning it can be a good time to buy them. As always, do your homework.

Qualities of an all-star share

All-stars are high quality, long-term shares that have competitive advantage and whose dividends display ongoing growth. Yet what typifies 'quality' in a share?

I want to take you back to Chapter 1 and my *Ford v Ferrari* example to talk further about the concept of quality and what makes you money. In the film, Henry Ford II had a real issue with the success of Ferrari. Even though the company went bust and was bought by Fiat, Ferrari had something that Ford craved – prestige and performance. More than 50 years on, Ferrari is still one of the most sought-after luxury cars and one of the most lucrative investments in the car market. Ferraris are often tagged with the name 'supercars', and it's because they have 'quality'.

Ford beat Ferrari in the 1966 Le Mans and in the next three years, the cars that raced and won this historic race became valuable to collectors.

- The Ford GT40 Mk 11 that won in 1966 attracted a price of US$9.795 million in 2017 at auction.

- In comparison, a 1966 Ferrari 365 P2 that raced in the 1966 Le Mans is currently valued at around £25 million or US$32.5 million.

Alternatively, if you compare the popular Ford Mustang and the Ferrari California, both produced in 1966:

- 1966 Mustang: Ford produced almost 610,000 and the high spec hard top retailed at US$2713. The current top price achieved for that car is US$26,800.

- 1966 Ferrari California: Ferrari produced 14 at a retail price of US$21,000. The top sold price to date is US$4.4 million and the average price is between US$750,000 and $1.1 million.

The Ferrari would have made you considerably more money as an investment.

The Ferrari was exclusive, had higher barriers to entry (a higher purchase price), but offered prestige, the famous red colour, the prancing horse insignia, European style and was handmade. This equated to a much higher capital gain, even if the dividends were lower (maybe you drove the car less). The Ford Mustang was cheaper, but you drove it a lot, similar to achieving a short-term higher dividend. In the long term the more expensive car, which is perceived to be higher quality, was the better investment.

The *Ford v Ferrari* example is aimed at showing you how different companies are. Although both companies manufactured cars and won at Le Mans, comparing them is like comparing a cubic zirconia to a diamond. One brings short-term joy at a lower expense and the other costs a lot more but delivers the best money-making result. Quality is what you're looking for when you're buying shares.

Of course, there's more to share investing, but quality is as much about perception (until proven otherwise) as it is about the numbers. It takes a long time to change the narrative around a company, so you should always check and compare the numbers – that is, the growth in dividends – to ensure you're buying and holding the correct shares.

In the appendix, I take a more in-depth look at quality and cultures in companies in my analysis of the US industrial giant Boeing and its 737 Max, and Australia's CSL.

Chapter summary

- ► Dividends don't lie. Cash payments and consistent growth in dividends is an optimum goal for investors.

- ► Beware of the dividend trap: high dividend yields and payouts are often a harbinger of lower share prices and a cut in the dividends.

- ► Cyclical shares are more prone to changes in the dividends over time.

- ► Quality shares matter for long-term investors.

Indirect investing: spoilt for choice or a minefield?

Did you know that the number eight is the luckiest number, financially, in Chinese culture? The Chinese pronunciation of eight is 'ba', which sounds like 'fa', meaning to make a fortune. It's apt then that this chapter, Chapter 8, is all about ensuring your money is working the best way it possibly can.

So far, the *Shareplicity* journey has been about how to invest directly into shares, but this chapter is about indirect investing. Direct investing, if you remember, is owning shares in your own name and constructing a share portfolio. Indirect investing involves having a third party invest your money on your behalf – perhaps in the form of passive funds (ETFs) or actively managed funds such as LICs, LITs and mFunds.

However, everything you have learnt is just as important if you own shares indirectly through any of the many investment funds/vehicles. Most investors don't have a proper understanding of what the funds they're buying into offer and can deliver. Too often investors are lured by the jargon, the narrative of recent high performance returns and fancy presentations. If you choose to be a non-direct share investor you still need a reasonable understanding of what you have selected.

Different types of investment funds

Investment funds come in a variety of different shapes and colours, or, in finance speak, structures. Some are known as managed funds and include listed investment companies (LICs), listed investment trusts (LITs), and mFunds (a financial instrument to give you access to unlisted funds). Then there are passive funds, known as other financial instruments, like exchange traded funds (ETFs) and exchange traded products (ETPs).

For our purposes, it's best not to become bogged down in the definitions of the structures, as they're all designed as vehicles for you to invest in. The main difference is in the tax treatment of a LIC and a LIT. LICs are companies and LITs are trusts (like ETFs). LITs make distributions from the underlying shares they invest in. They don't pay franked dividends but do pass on the franking credits to shareholders. LICs pay out of retained profits at the discretion of the board.

'Open ended' funds like unit trusts issue and cancel shares depending on the demand for units, meaning they have to buy or sell the underlying shares to meet the change in demand for the trust.

A 'closed end' trust or company lists only a fixed amount of shares that can be bought and sold; the amount of shares available doesn't fluctuate with the changes in demand for the shares. However, these vehicles, because they're closed, can trade at a discount or premium to the net tangible asset value (NTA) of the underlying shares held in the vehicle.

This is so much to consider when all you want is to buy into a vehicle that gives you exposure to shares, and a group of shares that will make you money!

Table 8.1 shows a summary of the key characteristics from Morningstar for those of you who are interested in how the structures vary between the vehicles.

TABLE 8.1 Summary of the difference between LITs, LICs and unlisted managed funds

	Listed investment trust	Listed investment company	Unlisted managed fund
Unit of value	Units	Shares	Units
Funds under management	Closed ended (raised through IPO)	Closed ended (raised through IPO)	Open ended (subject to daily inflows and outflows)
Trading	ASX through broker	ASX through broker	Direct application to custodian, platform or mFund
Pricing	Determined by market; may trade at a discount or premium to NTA	Determined by market; may trade at a discount or premium to NTA	Proportion of net assets
Distribution/ dividend	All income (underlying dividends and realised capital gain) is paid out through distributions	Dividend may be paid out of retained profits, subject to board discretion	All income (underlying dividends and realised capital gain) is paid out through distributions
Taxation	Distributions are subject to the tax rate of the underlying investor	Pays tax at the corporate tax rate, therefore may pass franking credits to the underlying investor	Distributions are subject to the tax rate of the underlying investor
Capital gains tax	Individual investors may be eligible for CGT discount for underlying investments held for longer than 12 months	Corporate entities are generally not eligible for CGT discount, although certain LICs may receive an ATO concession to pass this benefit onto shareholders	Individual investors may be eligible for CGT discount for underlying investments held for longer than 12 months

Source: ©2020 Morningstar, Inc. All Rights Reserved. Reproduced with permission.

Why ETFs are so popular

ETFs are passive investment products and are the fastest growing category of investment vehicle. As the name suggests, an ETF is listed on the stock exchange, and replicates (mirrors) the performance of a predetermined or designated group of shares, bonds or different securities (financial instruments, including currencies, cash or commodities).

For many investors they are a great choice. Here's why they're so appealing and what benefits they can provide you.

Let's say you want to achieve the same returns as the ASX 200: all you need to do is buy an ETF that represents the underlying shares in the ASX 200 and you'll see the listed price move in the same direction as the index and receive dividend payments corresponding to the underlying shares.

The ETF allows you to buy the index of shares at a very low cost (0.09 per cent or lower) and receive the income so you don't have to directly buy the shares yourself. An ETF is a no-frills vehicle to invest in that can be readily traded on the share market.

To understand the appeal of ETFs, no-one probably said it better about what's at stake than the founder and grandfather of ETFs, Jack Bogle, who passed away in January 2019. According to his obituary in *The New York Times*, in 1976 Bogle stated, 'In investing, you get what you don't pay for. Costs matter. Returns are uncertain but fees are not. So intelligent investors will use low-cost index funds to build a diversified portfolio of stocks and bonds, and they will stay the course. And they won't be foolish enough to think that they consistently outsmart the market'.

Like everything, technology is having a major impact on the finance industry and that's here to stay. The impact of technology is most evident in the growth in funds under management in ETFs.

There's no indication that ETF platforms are slowing in popularity and growth in funds under management. One agency estimated that the global ETF market reached US$5.57 trillion in the first quarter of 2019! Although ETFs are a newer product for Australian investors, there are many good reasons why ETFs have grown in popularity and why the market will continue to expand.

(If you want to find out more about this topic, have a look at the keynote address from the President and CEO of State Street Global Advisers at the FT Future of Asset Management Summit 2019 in London.)

How ETF products differ from managed funds

ETFs work on the basis that over the long term a share picker or active fund manager (LITs, LICs and mFunds) cannot outperform an index, particularly when the costs are taken into account.

The easiest way to appreciate the difference is that an active fund manager makes the picks depending on the mandate. The key to knowing what you're buying into is understanding the mandate, and that's when all the jargon of the finance industry can be overwhelming. Here are just a few types of managed fund mandates:

- **Long/short absolute return.** The fund manager can do just about whatever they want to make money. This usually comes with high risk. You might make a lot of money or lose a lot, but there are always basic management fees and sometimes additional performance fees.

- **Australian shares that return, let's say, 3 per cent above the cash rate (0.75 per cent).** This is most likely an index-hugging fund that fulfils the mandate if it delivers a return of above 3.75 per cent, even if the index goes up by 10 per cent or more.

- **A small capitalisation or big capitalisation share fund.** The fund manager picks either smaller shares or larger shares. The performance mandate might vary.

- **A global shares fund.** The fund manager can pick any stocks depending on the mandate from around the globe.

All these examples of managed funds have management fees attached. If you spend even a little time looking at the ASX list (refer Table 8.1), I believe you'll be quite surprised that a lot of the managed funds that come in the form of LITs and LICs are not making much money. Even in the bull market of 2019, some lost as much as 27 per cent in value. Stock picking is fun but it's also hard to be right all the time, even for the so-called experts.

An ETF, in comparison, takes the hassle out of how to choose between fund managers and what the impact of the costs will be. You merely decide on the sector and group of shares that you want. You can buy more over time and set-and-forget.

Managing your managed fund

I have nothing against managed funds – they have a time and place – but costs matter. Investors need to regularly review whether a fund is charging too much. Often investors think that if the fund is making a positive return, then they're doing okay. However, this is not what you should aim for; a positive return may not be what's reasonable and what's possible.

As a benchmark, here are some numbers to give you an idea of what has been achieved historically. According to marketindex. com.au, the Australian share market has returned an average of 13 per cent p.a. since 1900, including dividends.

There have been 23 negative years (19 per cent of the total period), 96 positive years (81 per cent) and 48 years (40 per cent) that returned between 10 and 20 per cent p.a.

While history isn't a reliable or accurate picture of the future and returns are being reduced because we're living in a lower-growth, lower-interest-rate environment, it doesn't mean that you should accept anything less than what the market average is returning for your share funds. A reasonable and conservative benchmark is an 7 to 10 per cent return p.a. with dividends. If your managed funds are not keeping pace it might be time to review and reset. Taking a loss is never easy, but the cost of remaining with an underperformer is greater.

Here are some real examples: in 2019, the ASX 200 total return including dividends from 3 January 2019 to 3 January 2020 was 24.22 per cent. If you owned an ETF you would have received almost exactly that return and if you had a managed fund you should check whether your fund did or didn't achieve that return. If it didn't, you would have paid the fees regardless.

That's one side of the argument for ETFs and against actively managed funds. The converse argument is that active managed funds can theoretically lose you less money when markets are falling. I stress the term 'theoretically'. If the fund's mandate is to outperform the ASX 200 and the ASX 200 falls by 5 per cent one year, if your fund falls by 4.5 per cent that means the active fund manager has outperformed the index. Actively managed funds can lose you money whether it's in the good or bad years.

How to select an active or passive fund

So, all roads seem to lead back to the wise words from Jack Bogle: costs matter. There will be instances when an ETF isn't appropriate and generally it's fair to say that some funds are better over some periods. However, even the mighty guru Warren Buffett has struggled to perform in recent years.

There are almost as many fund mandates (what they invest in) and benchmarks (a specific level of performance that can be numerical or an index) for these structures as there are funds available. This means you need to establish some selection criteria.

Here are two essential factors that will help determine the easiest and most efficient way to make a decision about which funds to run with, passive or active:

1. **Cost:** the costs of the funds and the hidden fees for the recommendation, if you use an adviser.

2. **Performance:** do they give a minimum (after cost) long-term performance in line with the share market? (Assuming you're not targeting a non-market correlation – that is, a hedge fund.)

When I was researching this chapter, I was overwhelmed by how much choice is out there. So much choice: how could anyone possibly make a reasonable decision? This is why so many people rely on some form of adviser, but you need to keep in mind that advisers have their own agendas.

Using an adviser

If you're new to the investment game and want to find a suitable fund for your savings, how or where do you start? It may vary depending on your age, or you may ask a friend or a relative or someone you think is in the know. Maybe you have been recommended an adviser – a stockbroker, financial planner, wealth manager or maybe even an accountant – to help you start your investment process. You want your savings to work for you and it seems only reasonable to go to 'an expert' who will filter through the current 371 options in the ETFs, mFunds, LICs and LITs categories.

I went down this path some 17 years ago ('What type of an expert is she?', I hear you scoff). At the time, for a variety of reasons including having been out of Australia for 14 years, I felt unable to manage my own money so I went to the so-called experts when I moved back from London. The experience taught me a lot. Ultimately, I became so frustrated with the advice, the lack of performance (in making me money) and the cost that I took the brave step of selling everything at the start of the 2008 crash and starting all over on my own. I know I'm blowing my own trumpet here, but as a divorced mother with a young son that took some guts, yet I had to be prudent about determining the right investment road map for my son and me.

So I speak with some authority about the investment funds available to you, what are possibly the best ways to invest your money indirectly and how not to get 'ripped off'.

A story about advisers and clients

This story may go some way to explaining the problems between passive and actively managed funds. In 1999, I was in Switzerland at a purpose-built facility for executives of a major European bank, where employees gathered from around the world to partake in a ten-day compulsory course on the bank's global funds management business. I had made a career move from stockbroking and was now a client adviser for rich people.

Having come from the world of institutional stockbroking, I was a square peg in a round hole. By my own admission I have never been suited to working for very large institutions with a heavily bureaucratic structure; I'm too cynical, ask too many questions and like to work independently. Suffice to say, that side of my personality came to the fore at this course.

The bank I was working for had done very well over the years from investing its clients' funds into the in-house actively managed funds. It had groups of specific, professionally trained experts who analysed the share, bond and currency markets and bought shares or securities in these sectors in structures for the clients, called funds. The funds had specific mandates: they aimed to outperform a benchmark (usually a share index) and the clients invested in the fund based on the benchmarks as set out by the fund managers.

The bank I now worked for was similar to the clients I had looked after in my stockbroking career. One of my aims had been to avoid ripping them off with a bad deal; if I looked after my clients, they in turn would continue to do business with me. This path was not always so easy to navigate when my job entailed making money for my employer, who in turn made money from selling deals. If I refused to sell a deal (which I once did), that was not good for my employer.

The shoe was now on the other foot and my new clients were what we called 'high net worth individuals' – people with a few million available to invest in the bank's managed funds.

The course I attended was designed to educate us on the optimal ways to invest our clients' money. It was, and remains, a fairly standard model; banks funnel their clients' money into the in-house fund management products and earn a nice fund management fee. (The Banking Royal Commission has resulted in an about-turn on this model of banks selling their funds management businesses.)

Looking back, I was ignorant or stupidly brave when I queried the wisdom of the bank in feeding all the client funds into the in-house actively managed funds. I questioned the CEO of our group publicly about why the bank was not moving into the area of ETFs. I had all the answers for him: 'We could asset allocate our clients' money effectively across a multitude of sectors, countries and markets in a low-cost and efficient way'.

My suggestion was definitely not appreciated and I was politely reminded that was not the bank's business model. The model was to provide actively managed funds for its clients. In addition, of course, the reason the CEO wanted to retain the managed funds was because it was a nice fee earner. Although my solution would have benefitted my clients, it would also have eroded the bank's profits and long-standing business model.

Can you see the problem for banks and financial managers/advisers? In order to provide an advisory service to their clients, they need to generate an income, either through a fee or a vehicle like a managed fund, which in turn generates income.

Like going to the doctor, financial advice isn't free. So, the questions you need to ask yourself are:

- Am I paying the correct amount for the advice and are the fees appropriate?
- Is there any chance that the adviser is potentially conflicted by serving both my best interests and their own?

As it transpired, I did not stay long at that bank and, 20 years on, I think it's fair to say that I was well ahead of the curve. Those low-cost ETFs that I was advocating for in 1999 have taken the world by storm.

Indirect investment options for your money

Australia has been a veritable gold, platinum and diamond mine combined, metaphorically speaking, for the finance sector, particularly over the last 20 years. It has been a perfect positive storm for the finance and investment industry – we have one of the largest pools of superannuation monies, 28 years of uninterrupted economic growth, a booming property market and an affluent ageing population. Mix this together with falling interest rates and there has been literally a wall of money looking for a home to make a return. The industry responded in kind to this demand and has created a plethora of investment funds for us to invest in.

I discovered an excellent summary of all the funds available for investors on the ASX website, including the performance, category, size, volume traded and growth in funds under management. As shown in Table 8.2, the list is extensive, particularly in the categories of ETPs (or ETFs), mFunds and LICs and LITs.

In Chapter 5, I touched on Australian REITs (Goodman Group, Dexus and Charter Hall, for example) and the infrastructure category (Sydney Airport and Transurban) as part the ASX 30 express. I consider these to be appropriate in the direct share investing category.

TABLE 8.2: Summary chart of the different funds listed on the ASX

Category	ETPs	mFunds	LICs and LITs	AREITs	Infrastructure
Market cap ($bn)	60.2	1.1	52.0	155.0	91.7
Total number	208	114	49	49	8

Minimising costs and fees

In my story about advisers above, I explained how the bank made good earnings from managing funds. It's the same in Australia; managed funds work off a fee-based system.

Financial planners, stockbrokers and accountants also usually receive a fee for placing your money into specific managed funds. They're what could be termed the intermediaries, who have relationships with the fund management companies. The advisers receive a referral fee and the fund managers receive the fund's inflow – it's a win–win for both of them.

What do fees mean for your savings?

I'm going to let you in on a couple of big secrets that most advisers and fund managers don't sufficiently explain.

1. Most active share funds don't outperform the share market indices over the long term (the benchmarks they're set against); worse still, many lose clients' money, even when the market they're investing in is going up.

2. Your performance – that is, the money you make – gets eroded by costs. It takes a superhuman active fund manager to consistently make you money that covers the cost of fees of many of the managed funds.

Have a look back at Chapter 5: in the same way as we all need to take a look under the bonnet (assess a share in a bigger context), we also need to have a much closer inspection of how our investments are being managed. Beware of the fat-cat fee-takers.

You'll find an excellent tool known as the 'Managed funds fee calculator' on the ASIC website (moneysmart.gov.au) that allows you to input all your savings and fees for your managed funds to see the impact of costs.

For our purpose I have constructed three alternatives and only changed the fees to match the different investment products available to investors, to give you a glimpse into what costs do to your investment performance. The findings may shock you or at the very least trigger some alarm bells about where your savings are invested or where you're thinking of investing. Even as a long-term participant in investing I was truly shocked by the results. The time value or compounding of the costs is as bad as the compounding of savings is good.

Compounding example: assumptions

► You invest $10,000 initially and $500 every month thereafter for 30 years.

► You earn a compound rate of 7 per cent p.a. and all the dividends are reinvested.

► The total before costs would deliver you a savings pool of $660,849.

However, if I change the cost imposts from the different fees charged depending on the type of product, you'll see how dramatic the impact is on the final savings pool.

Note: this is purely an example. Some managed funds may not even make an average 7 per cent annual return and some advisers recommend their clients take out life and disability insurance as well, which is another cost.

Compounding example: results after 30 years

1. An ETF fund with an annual cost of 0.09 per cent delivers you $648,620 after fees of $12,229.

2. A managed fund with an annual fee of 2 per cent delivers you $441,867 after fees of $218,982.

3. A managed fund with an annual fee of 2 per cent and a 1 per cent annual adviser's fee delivers you $365,100 after fees of $295,749.

The higher costs and fees dramatically erode your savings. The second and third option can erode your end savings pool by as much as 45 per cent after 30 years. In an era when we're all living and working longer, I'm quite certain this isn't an outcome anyone wants.

Just in case you think I have a penchant for bashing managed funds and advisers, I want to emphasise that all of this information is in the public domain and the Banking Royal Commission has revealed the extent of fee gouging. It's one of the reasons for AMP's business problems (see Chapter 7).

The example does reflect very clearly that if you're being charged high fees, you'll be forsaking substantial future income. By halving the management costs of your fund from 2 per cent to 1 per cent over your lifetime you could halve the fees you pay.

With all the investment details remaining equal – a 7 per cent p.a. annual return – the ETF was the best product to make you the most money.

In the industry, there's an ongoing battle between the advisers and the active fund management industry against those that develop and provide ETF products to investors. On one hand you have the option of an expert managing your money (an active stock picker) and on the other you have a low-cost solution that statistically provides the long-term market performance of whatever the ETF is tracking.

Note: A number of specialist online platforms have evolved to provide lower-cost alternatives for investors to seek out financial advice. The growth in popularity of these platforms has come from the breakdown of the traditional pathways for wealth management in the banks. As with any platform or advisory option, you should always do your homework and understand the costs involved.

Next, Chapter 9 explores all the different ways to create or develop a share investment portfolio.

Chapter summary

► A set-and-forget approach isn't always sensible. You need to review your funds (but chopping and changing can be expensive).

► Check the management and adviser costs and see if you can improve on them, as lower fees will materially benefit your savings pool over time.

► Don't be afraid to ask your adviser lots of questions; investing isn't a black and white exercise.

► Don't be afraid to sell underperforming funds; some funds just don't make it and, like shares, they can become 'death stars' and eventually wind up. In some worst-case scenarios you may not receive all your money; although rare, it does happen.

► I think you'll be hearing more on the issue of high-cost, underperforming managed funds, so watch this space with interest and meanwhile consider the ETF options that are available.

9

Building the best portfolio for you

This is finally where the rubber hits the road: it's time to put the pieces of the share investment puzzle together. We are all individuals and have different aspirations, needs, wants, desires, goals, strengths, weaknesses and limitations, as well as different amounts of money/savings to invest. All these factors come into play in building the best portfolio for you. This chapter shows you how to construct a direct share investment portfolio and/or indirect portfolio via ETFs or managed funds.

Sticking with my growing theme (remember the vineyard?), I want you to envisage the creation of your share investment portfolio as the same as starting, developing and adapting a garden over time.

Like your garden (or one you like to visit), do the plants yield the growth, flowers, shade, shelter and enjoyment you seek? Is the garden resilient over time or does it need to adapt? Does it use too many resources or take up too much time? The same applies to your share portfolio: nothing is set in stone, but planning for the future at the outset makes all the difference.

Seventeen years ago, I began two journeys: one in personal investment and one in gardening, managing my own funds to live off and becoming a gardener for the first time. My garden has grown but is constantly in need of maintenance to meet the changing conditions; some plants die, some need trimming, new additions need to be planted and weeds need to be removed. I've planted more succulent and native plants, as the English plants I put in originally just couldn't cope with the warmer and drier conditions! With the benefit of hindsight, I would have designed and changed the original plantings.

My share portfolio has also needed shaping and additional 'planting' over the years. I have needed to change and adapt it along the way in response to my changing circumstances and those of the investment world. The lower-for-longer interest rate scenario has eroded the efficacy of cash deposits and some of the once-core blue chip companies have lost some of their shine.

So, to get started, go through the eight points below for planning your 'best' portfolio. Then you can mix and match from the portfolios that I outline later in this chapter, which are based on commitment required, level of risk and age.

The eight-point plan for creating your share portfolio

Planning prevents piss-poor performance. I love this statement. It was the catchcry for my son's team during his school rowing seasons and it's good general advice. It applies to many things from sport to finance and everything in between.

Armed with your new knowledge from *Shareplicity*, you can now plan for your investment portfolio or how you'll adapt what you already have. It's never too late to weed and prune what you've got or invest in some new shares!

Planning the 'best' investment portfolio for you will require a little preparation but nothing too arduous. Here is a go-to list of points to consider when starting out. The same list can be used each year as a check to make sure you're on track.

1. Know yourself.
2. Have clear goals.
3. Prepare to take risks.
4. Exercise control.
5. Do regular reviews.
6. Stick to the 80:20 rule.
7. Use reporting systems.
8. Be mindful of costs.

Below I flesh out the details for these steps.

1. Know yourself

This requires a good, honest look at yourself. Have you ever in your life bitten off more than you could chew? I know I have. So to plan your best portfolio, start by seeing where you fit on this checklist:

- How much time can you commit? A lot (weekly), some (monthly) or very little (annually)?

- Is your knowledge base low, medium or high? Your knowledge will have increased after you've read this book!

- How much experience do you have? None, some or a lot? For example, I have 'a lot', my son has close to 'none' and 'some' can vary between buying a share here or there and farming out all your money to managed funds or ETFs. The more experience you have, the better equipped you'll be.

► Are you prepared to spend time reading and learning more? I read daily, but then investing has become a vocation and a passion. I used to find the weekend financial paper, or the finance, money or wealth sections of the major papers, a good place to start to build up a knowledge base while avoiding information overload. Online analytics and financial news and data services can also be helpful, but tread carefully, as you need to distinguish between trading and investing tips (as per Chapter 2).

Your answers to these questions are very personal and will help to determine whether you fit into one of the three portfolio groups I outline in the following sections – low, medium or high maintenance – no matter what age you are.

2. Have clear goals

We all want to make money, but as I discussed in Chapter 8, it's useful to have a benchmark, whether you invest in shares directly or indirectly through passive (ETFs) or managed funds (LITs and LICs). A benchmark isn't a number you must or will achieve but rather a goalpost to keep in sight to check if you're pursuing the right strategy. In our low-return world, it's unrealistic to expect the historical total returns (capital and income) of 13 per cent p.a. A goal of between 7 and 10 per cent p.a. is more realistic. Some years will be higher or lower, but an average 7 per cent p.a. return with income reinvested will more than double your money in ten years.

You also need a savings and investment plan: decide how much you want to invest at the start, what's affordable and whether you can continue to make contributions over time. If you can contribute, it's worth considering the timing from both a market and cost perspective. Try to buy your chosen shares when the share market falls ('sells off') or when the share's price falls (is 'sold down'). Also, save up your money so you have a larger amount in your bank before you buy the shares to invest, so as to reduce the costs (the cost of share trading is proportionally higher if the amount invested is smaller).

3. Prepare to take risks

This is probably the most challenging concept for new and even some seasoned investors to understand. To achieve a high investment return you need to take more risk, meaning you need to buy into certain types of shares or investment funds that can make you more money but can also lose you more money. On a scale, shares are riskier than bonds but a lot less risky than trading commodities or currencies. Small companies with less liquidity are more risky than larger companies with higher liquidity. Resource and gold (cyclical) shares are possibly more risky than defensive shares – that is, companies whose earnings are stable in spite of what is happening in the economy, such as health care companies and consumer discretionary stocks like Woolworths. It depends on where the companies generate their earnings.

Most of us don't properly understand risk until we have been burnt, as in suffered a real and material loss. Experience is the best teacher for understanding risk. Your risk will also vary depending on your age; more risk can be taken when you're younger (as you have a longer time frame to recover a loss). However, the lower-for-longer interest rate theme means you need to take more risk-growth stocks for a longer period in your life (as we're all living longer).

In order to reduce risk when investing, the concept is to diversify the savings (monies invested) across different shares or platforms – managed funds or ETFs. In this way, you maintain investment exposure but aim to ensure that no one share or fund represents too much of your savings should something go wrong.

4. Exercise control

Some investors have a greater predilection for trading, punting or basically gambling. That is, they want to make a quick profit and think a nice punt on a share will make them a couple of grand. Of course, this is possible sometimes but not likely or probable all the time. If you have this type of personality, you need to put a cap on how much of your money you'll use to punt or trade with. Very few people can successfully trade their way to wealth. With any portfolio you adopt, you need to ensure you spread your cash across a few shares or funds. This is known as 'not placing all your eggs in one basket'. It will help to manage the risk of your investments.

5. Do regular reviews

Depending on how involved you are with your portfolio, a review can be done quarterly, six-monthly or annually. If you're not trading, it's preferable not to be swept up into the daily noise of the markets and volatility (shares prices moving up and down). The reviews can include:

- Are my investment choices working? If not, why not and should I change my strategy?

- Should I take some profits on some shares?

- Should I sell any shares or funds? Are there any capital killers or death stars in the portfolio?

- Are there emerging secular market trends (long-term growth in sectors like 5G wireless technology, health care and alternative meat products, for example) I should seek exposure to?

- Are there any risks from changing regulations or competition?

- Do I have too many shares in the portfolio? Selling is as important as buying: avoid the long tail of the tensaggers.

- Will I spend or reinvest my dividend income? It's always preferable to increase your long-term returns to invest the dividend income, but be sure not to keep buying into shares or funds that have any question marks over their long-term performance (remember the AMP story in Chapter 7).

Be careful of investing in too many small shares during a bull market. Most shares rise in a bull market; it's only when a bear market arrives that you can see which of your emperors (your small shares) have no clothes, and are not as good as you thought they were.

6. Stick to the 80:20 rule

This is relevant to any portfolio investing and it refers to the basic concept that 80 per cent of your performance will be achieved from 20 per cent of the exposure. For example, if you have ten shares in your portfolio, more likely than not 20 per cent or two of those shares will account for 80 per cent of the increase in the value of the portfolio. Alternatively, if you recall the statistics from Chapter 8, since 1900 the Australian share market has recorded 19 per cent negative years and 81 per cent positive years, meaning the good years outweigh the bad years by a factor of 4. Therefore, it's preferable to remain invested to achieve the long-term goals. The share market goes up eight out of ten years, so unless it's a dire situation or you're nearing retirement, hang on in there. Optimism outweighs pessimism in share investing.

7. Use reporting systems

Come tax time you'll benefit from having in place efficient reporting systems to log the dividend income and change in the value from one year to the next. Some advisers or platforms like

CommSec, which I use, have reporting systems, but it's always sensible to weigh up the costs against the benefit.

8. Be mindful of costs

I think it's a reasonable assumption that most of us haven't really come to grips with the costs of share investing and the best ways to minimise them. This is relevant in a low-interest-rate world where costs (as shown in Chapter 8) can have an extremely bad impact on the money you make in the future. (As the returns on shares drop, costs increase proportionally using traditional models.)

If you've already invested, you may need some courage to assess the costs and restructure your portfolio. If you're an avid trader you need to and should include the costs of trading in your calculations; you may not have made as much money as you thought. If you're a new investor, well, the world is your oyster as there's now so much choice available in terms of low-cost products such as ETFs and low-cost share-trading platforms. It's particularly noticeable if you're investing small amounts into shares. I experienced this with my son, when I helped him put a small portfolio of shares together. As the capital invested shrinks, the percentage cost erodes the performance, particularly for amounts under $2000 per share.

Establishing what kind of share investor you are

I give you some sample portfolios later in this chapter (see Figures 9.1 and 9.2), but how useful they are will depend on how much money or savings you have to invest. Let's first identify the type of investor you are. I have split these into five general categories, and while there are probably more out there, I'm quite sure you can easily fit into one of these.

First-time investor

Are you a student or a young professional saving for a holiday or housing deposit? You can start a portfolio with as little as $500. The less money you have, the simpler and risk-free the investment should be. It's just not feasible (from a cost standpoint) or reasonable to think that you should buy five to ten separate shares at $100 each. For anything less than, let's say $2000, as a first-time investor you should probably only consider buying one ETF to start, like an ETF that replicates the ASX 200 share index, for example. You can keep contributing to that until it reaches a critical mass of $5000. You could then consider adding some shares, but anything less than $1000 per share is just not worth it. Better to keep adding to the ETF fund and grow that.

For savings or money of $10,000 plus you can start to look at the model portfolios that suit your age, risk tolerance and commitment level.

Inheritance monies

Inheriting shares or money is sometimes emotionally challenging, as you may put undue pressure on yourself not to make a mistake and lose any of the money. You may feel conflicted about selling the shares you have inherited to change the portfolio. You may also be a new investor and then the task is more daunting. Depending on the size of the inheritance it may be wise to seek tax advice. Keep to the script, remember costs, don't invest in anything you don't understand, and consider how the money can be best invested.

Can you add the money to your superannuation or through a self-managed super fund? If you're anxious about the risks, start with the low risk, low maintenance sample portfolios later in this chapter. As your confidence grows and your knowledge base increases you can select more shares.

Divorce settlement

Investing money from a divorce settlement can be an emotionally fraught situation, particularly for women who may not have much financial experience. The wounds of the divorce are compounded with the fear of the unknown. Now, I'm not a divorce counsellor, but I have been there with a young son, starting out in a new town (I relocated back to Sydney from London). I know it can be daunting, but gently, gently:

- Be kind to yourself, step back, take a deep breath and don't rush any decisions.

- Try to get some good tax advice; you want a good family accountant if it's a reasonable settlement amount.

- Think about how much you need to live off and what needs to be invested. When it comes to the investment aspect, refer to the section about costs in Chapter 8. It's more likely than not that your money will be better invested in a low risk, low maintenance portfolio than anything more costly with an adviser.

You won the lottery

Having never won the lottery I don't know how it feels, but I do often hear of people losing it all. So, if you win the lottery or the equivalent (as in, you receive a large lump sum of money), then you need to be prudent when it comes to investing and spending the money. In my time I have received sizeable bonuses as remuneration for my work in London. I can assure you I was very disciplined about best using the lump sums either by paying off my mortgage or investing the money in shares. It's too easy when we're younger (or older!) to not save or manage wisely any lump sums we receive. It's so easy to spend and so much harder to make the money we need as we age.

Depending on your level of financial knowledge, I suggest any lump sums should be properly allocated across a number of shares and ETFs including overseas ETFs. As lump sums are usually bigger amounts it's important to diversify; so, depending on your ability, knowledge and experience, many of the sample portfolios (see Figures 9.1 and 9.2) would work.

Unhappy existing investor

I know how this feels, and it's not always easy to have the conversation with yourself or an adviser about what isn't working and how to fix the problems. It will come down to you identifying what isn't working for you and then putting in place a plan to redress the situation. A few considerations:

- It's never too late to sell; holding on to the tensaggers or the losers isn't a winning strategy. The losing shares just never recover to your purchase price, so bite the bullet, sell and invest your money in a share or an ETF that will make you money.

- Don't be afraid to change an adviser or sell a managed fund; the world is changing and that includes share investments. Waiting for the pot of gold at the end of the rainbow isn't sensible. I suggest you follow the model portfolios that suit your age and disposition.

Examples of portfolios

You can mix and match the six portfolio models I offer below to create your best portfolio depending on your commitment level and risk tolerance (see Figures 9.1 and 9.2). In the following section I also give you three examples of portfolios you could build based on your age. I also provide a sample portfolio of a medium maintenance/medium risk portfolio that could be good for a new investor. If you want to do direct investing, see the 12-point plan for creating a direct share portfolio.

Note: These are all examples only; they're not recommendations. They are suggestions, to give you some idea of how to structure a portfolio and what weightings and risk profile are possible. Everyone is different and some of you may want to be more or less involved. Whatever choices you make, just do your research and try to fit the style of your portfolio to meet your needs and abilities. Investing is as much about having fun as it is about making money!

The sample portfolios are based on how much time you want to spend share-wrangling:

- ► low maintenance – 80 to 100 per cent ETFs, up to 20 per cent shares
- ► medium maintenance – 50 to 60 per cent ETFs, 40 to 50 per cent shares
- ► high maintenance – up to 40 per cent ETFs, 60 per cent or more shares.

The portfolios are then built on how much risk you're prepared to wear. In a nutshell, risk is how much you stand to make or lose in terms of shares. The higher the risk – from high-growth funds or shares – the more money you can potentially make, but also the more you can potentially lose. A Swiss wealth manager once told me, for example, that her firm's pure share funds fell 50 per cent or more during the 2008 GFC, depending on the mix of shares, while the balanced funds (those that held a mixture of bonds, shares and property) only fell some 17 per cent.

FIGURE 9.1: Investing based on how much time you want to spend managing your portfolio

LOW MAINTENANCE	MEDIUM MAINTENANCE	HIGH MAINTENANCE
80 to 100 per cent ETFs	50 to 60 per cent ETFs	Up to 40 per cent ETFs
Up to 20 per cent shares	40 to 50 per cent shares	60 per cent or more shares

FIGURE 9.2: Suggested portfolio of weightings and structure based on the amount of risk you want to take

LOW RISK	MEDIUM RISK	HIGH RISK/ HIGH GROWTH
Defensive shares, greater weighting to income	*Balance between growth and income*	*Large exposure to secular growth shares*
80% weighting ETFs: bonds, dividends, developed markets (Australia, USA and maybe Europe) high-quality REITs, gold	**50% weighting** ETFs: developed markets, less in bonds, dividends and income	**30–40% weighting** ETFs: emerging markets, trend ETFs like cannabis, IT, space and AI
20% weighting Quality/dividend champion shares like CSL, CBA, REA	**50% weighting** More quality shares with possibly some resource exposure, banks and technology	**60–70% weighting** Growth, technology, cyclicals (lithium) and emerging technologies

No-one's expecting a GFC moment, but it's prudent when you construct your portfolio to consider how much risk you can stomach and how you can 'de-risk' your investments. In the examples that follow I discuss some ETF products that provide exposure to more income-defensive (safer) investments to offset share exposure in a low risk portfolio. Hedge funds fall more into the high risk category and bond funds in the developed market (Australia, the USA, the UK) fall at the low risk end.

How your age may change your portfolio profile

Traditionally, professional advisers recommended that investors had investments in corporate bonds or fixed income equal to their age in years. For example, if you're 50 years old, 50 per cent of the total cash is invested in bonds. You can buy ETFs or managed funds that give you exposure to high quality corporate bonds and government bonds, however given the low-growth world, I would suggest the weightings should be lower.

Arguably anyone under 40 to 50 years old probably should maintain a high to full exposure to shares. Advisers recommended bonds and fixed income because they were considered as lower risk: in down markets the funds go down less than shares.

'Home offices' for wealthy families normally recommend a mix of one-third shares, one-third bonds and one-third property. ('Home office' is an expression used by investment managers to refer to wealthy families who pay a specialist to look after their investments and affairs.) With the help of ETF products and REITs you too can achieve such an asset allocation. However, I would suggest it's not appropriate for most of you, particularly younger investors. In my experience, this allocation is too conservative (risk-free) for anyone under 40 years old.

In your younger years, you want more growth (and possibly more risk) for two reasons:

1. The shares have the potential to go up more in a low-interest-rate world.

2. Some of the high-growth companies turn into the dividend champions that become some of the best long-term wealth creators.

My two portfolios

I have tried to structure my two portfolios with different mandates. I live off my investment portfolio and it has a much higher weighting to income (yield and growth). My superannuation portolio, on the other hand, has a much heavier growth slant.

In the investment portfolio, I have a select group of ten shares that deliver a reasonable income with good long-term growth prospects, and I don't own the major banks except Macquarie.

My superannuation portfolio is a mixture of:

- growth and technology shares
- defensive and quality shares (think health care related shares; some infrastructure shares)
- high quality REITs like Goodman Group.

They were all purchased a few years back to capture a mix of shares that had the capacity to generate secular growth (long-term non-cyclical trends), some with a higher yield and others with the ability to increase the yield and dividend payments over time. I also invest directly in US shares through the CommSec platform (other online platforms offer a similar service) and have done so for over three years. That has been quite a learning curve and takes a reasonable amount of time to read about and maintain. There's also a good splattering of technology/growth shares in the US portfolio. The aim is to invest in shares that become dividend champions and the leaders in the next ten years: think Apple, Microsoft or Google ten years ago.

My portfolios are fairly sophisticated because I have a lot of experience and knowledge. For beginner investors, however, the good news is that most of what I invest in can be captured in passive funds like ETFs and some managed funds.

Even if you decide to invest indirectly via an ETF or managed fund, it's important to have some understanding of the underlying exposure of shares or securities you're buying into. For example, if you buy an ETF for the ASX 200 and then buy some CSL, BHP and CBA shares, you need to be aware that you're increasing your exposure/weighting or money invested, as the ETF would have those three shares as the three largest holdings. There's nothing wrong with this, as by doubling up, so to speak, you can increase the money you make if you think CSL, BHP and CBA will rise more than the index. The technical term for this is 'alpha', meaning you can add certain shares to your ETF portfolio to increase the returns above the long-term market index.

Following are some possible portfolio mixes according to age.

20–40 years: low maintenance/high risk combination

For this age group, I suggest a selection of high-growth and major index share exposure through ETFs predominantly – a few high-quality shares. The aim is to invest as early as possible and keep adding to the share portfolio, while keeping costs down. There are a number of themes millennial investors and Gen Z are attracted to that can be captured in ETFs: these include ethical, ESG, sustainable funds, domestic and global; technology themes like global robotics and AI; and global cyber security. There are more listed in the USA with themes such as climate change and space captured in the ETFs, but you'll need a US share account.

40–65 years: medium maintenance/high to medium risk combination

In these two decades your involvement and ability to invest will depend on your work and family life commitments. Normally as we age there's more time to commit to our share portfolio, but this is a very personal decision based on confidence, commitment to reading and education as well as enjoyment. For some of you it might become a vocation and a passion, but at all times assess your limitations and manage the risk.

As you age, you may want to consider increasing your exposure to shares, products or securities that provide stable and reliable income streams or at least setting the stage for investing in those shares that can deliver those dividend streams in the future. Adding good quality REITs and maybe some exposure to corporate bond ETFs is a possibility as well. These also set the stage for securing a future income stream.

65 onwards: medium to high maintenance/low risk combination

This is probably the most challenging age demographic to comment on and will depend on whether you're already in this age group or structuring the portfolio for when you reach this demographic.

Someone in this age group asked me a couple of years back if they should sell their CBA shares. What a tough question, and a question that could never be answered in isolation. If you have held bank shares like CBA for years you have a difficult decision to make when it comes to selling them, because they produce high franked income for you. You're probably also sitting on a large capital gain. Try to avoid making a decision based on tax considerations. However, if you have made the tough decision to sell or at least partially sell such shares, ask yourself, can you afford to lose the income? Maybe it's better to potentially sacrifice a future capital gain or capital to maintain the income.

If you're still investing, think seriously about adding to these positions. Good portfolios manage the risk between shares. Try not to put too much in any one share, no matter how much you love it, and remember that even good companies go through tough times.

A simple 12-point plan for building a direct share portfolio

1. A reasonable allocation of shares is 5–10 per cent of your capital in any one share for a $10,000 to $25,000 share portfolio. As the amount invested grows, I suggest lowering the allocation per share to 3–5 per cent.

2. The larger the portfolio, the more you may want to consider a bond ETF and increased exposure to REITs, which are exposed to the optimal sectors of the property market, for growth and income.

3. The more you increase the weighting to a share, the more risk you're taking on (the more money you can make and the more money you can lose).

4. Avoid creating a portfolio with 40 plus shares – it's just too many.

5. Remember to do the weeding and cull the losers or the saggers. The money can be better invested in a share that is going up.

6. Take some profits along the way but keep your quality core holdings; the dividend champions will repay your original capital many times over in dividends received.

7. Remember that you're not performing against an index, although you will need to reassess your portfolio if you're not achieving the long-term returns of the market.

8. Be clear about what you're aiming to achieve; most of us will need growth and income as we're living longer in a low-interest-rate world.

9. Reinvest the dividend income if you can; it grows your wealth more effectively and allows the power of compounding.

10. Don't trade too much or allocate only a small amount to trading.

11. Watch and monitor the costs.

12. Make a commitment to stay informed and open-minded, and never say never.

Dow theory: using charts to time when you buy, sell or hold

I'm not a trader or a chartist but I do look at charts before I buy, and sometimes sell, a share. The chart may not give me all the information, but it can give me an idea of the share price trend. Remember that 'the trend is your friend'. Trying to pick the top or the bottom of a share price or a market is a mug's game; it's very hard to be spot on all the time. You can, however, improve your timing in buying and selling shares using charts, as they can confirm if the share is in a major upward or downward trend. Do you recall the Aristocrat Leisure and Speedcast charts in Chapter 4? Aristocrat is in an excellent long-term uptrend and

Speedcast has fallen off a cliff. Dow theory could have been applied in both cases to establish buy or sell signals.

Here's a good example of using a chart. Let's say you're thinking Speedcast has been oversold and that investors are just too negative. The company isn't going to go bust and you think it's so cheap you must buy it. There's no doubt the shares have been sold off but nobody has any idea whether the company will be a good money-maker off these lows. So, if you buy the shares, in many ways you're taking a punt.

Traders or investors who like to 'bottom fish' – buy sold-off, bombed-out shares (the left side of the valuation table in Chapter 4) – often use a chart to confirm that the share price has bottomed (won't fall any further). They check to see if the share price has been consolidating (moving sideways), if the recent lows haven't been breached and if the share is holding and making new highs.

Much of this technique is based on Dow theory, which was created a hundred years ago by Charles Dow. His premise was that everything (every bit of news) is discounted in the share price, so that you can look at the share price charts to obtain an indication of where the future price will go.

His theory was based on a vastly different US economy where the railroads were the kings and the Dow index was correlated to the Transport index, as the movement of traded goods was an indication of economic strength. Yet times have changed, and in 21st century investing the digital economy has changed that paradigm. Nevertheless, the Dow theory principles are still useful, even if they're not specifically correlated to the Dow and Transport indices.

Dow theory is based on a number of points:

1. Everything about a share or market is indicated in the chart.

2. The chart consists of the primary, secondary and minor trends, broadly meaning the annual, monthly and weekly price trend (up, down or sideways). The primary is the most important (is it up or down?), so looking at the secondary or minor trends will offer you a signal that there's an opportunity to take advantage of the primary trend.

3. There are three phases of the trends: accumulation (when there's more buying but still selling and the price is stabilising); public participation (when the public investors start to buy); followed by distribution (when the less informed are buying and there's often a blow-off top or bubble).

4. Volumes are a secondary indicator; good strong volumes are a positive confirmation of the bias up or down.

5. The theory also says that the trend will continue until an opposite force is applied (something either very negative or positive that changes the fundamentals of the share or market).

You can use a chart to assist you in buying or selling shares or ETFs. None of us want to buy at the top of a bubble, but we do want to time our entry or exit if we can. For example, I want to buy some CSL shares, but the price has already gone up 60 per cent in the last year. What should I do? Well, I know that at some stage the share will be sold off for whatever reason. When this occurs, I need to decide whether it's a primary event, if the upward trend is reversing, or if it's a secondary event.

I need to be patient: stand back and see how the price moves. Once the share price fall stops, see if it's going to move back upwards and wait until the chart gives the signal; that is, the price rises above the recent high, and then doesn't retrace to the recent low. You want a share price that sets higher lows and higher highs, not lower lows and lower highs.

The main takeaway point is that I don't use charts in isolation, but they can be a very useful tool to time when you enter or exit a market or share. It's my belief that using only charts or technical analysis isn't sufficient. In combination with all your other new knowledge, however, charts are extremely useful in either selling before a share falls off a cliff and becomes a sagger, or if the primary trend is in a strong upward trend, to assist in picking the winners.

A beginner's share portfolio

I can't tell you what shares to buy as I don't know you or your personal situation. However, what I can do is give you an idea of what a medium maintenance, medium risk portfolio might look like in my world as I write this book at the beginning of 2020.

As investing isn't a static exercise, what applies now could change by the time you read it: there could be a ' black swan event' (something totally unexpected) like the start of war in the Middle East, a global health pandemic like SARS or the coronavirus, or a strong pick-up of inflation in Australia or the USA. A 'green swan event' (a new term for a climate-related disaster) also has deleterious financial impacts. So, let's assume there are no black or green swans around the corner and that there's a reasonable sum available to allow for ten positions to be taken.

Theoretical medium risk/medium maintenance portfolio

Up to six ETFs, possibly including the following:

- an ETF that represents the ASX 200
- an ETF that represents the US S&P 500 or is invested in global major companies
- a technology theme capturing US and European tech shares
- a global emerging market
- possibly a gold or corporate bond ETF (this is better for income)
- a good quality REIT like Goodman Group or a real estate ETF.

Up to five shares, possibly including the following:

- three dividend champions
- one cyclical share like a resources or materials share (such as BHP)
- one trading punting share.

This selection assumes there's not a large lump sum and is for probably up to $10,000 or $20,000. With lower amounts I'd just pick two or three ETFs. With larger amounts you can have more shares, with the amount invested split roughly 50:50 between the ETFs and the shares. Just be aware that you might be doubling up with some of the shares in the ETF. There's nothing wrong with that but please make sure you're happy with the choice of higher exposure. Always reinvest the income if you can to optimise the returns over time.

Chapter summary

▶ Building the best portfolio for you brings all your new knowledge together.

▶ Use the knowledge, whether you invest directly or indirectly in shares.

▶ Plan your portfolio using the eight-point plan and review at least annually.

▶ Mix and match your portfolio according to your age, strengths and weaknesses.

▶ Don't be afraid to adapt the portfolio over time.

▶ Experience and confidence will improve your investment decisions.

▶ Use the 12-point plan as a reference to start, maintain and construct your direct share portfolio.

10

The wrap-up

Congratulations! You've completed the first steps on your journey to share investing and/or improving your share financial literacy. Whether you're a new or existing investor, the most important lesson for successful investing is remembering to invest in yourself. It may require some commitment to learning and understanding how and where your savings are being invested. This applies to any situation, whether you manage your own portfolios or you have outsourced your savings to a third party. No matter how much we rely on the experts, they're only human and can make mistakes, so it's always good to have an eye on the investment ball.

Time is precious and we all lead busy lives, but you won't regret the time you've spent learning more about share investing. The system has allowed too many investors to think they're either not capable or don't have enough knowledge. Even some knowledge will go a long way to improving your decision making and investing power.

I'm certain I'm not the only person who shudders at the awful tales of people being ripped off by promises of get-rich-quick schemes. These schemes come in many guises, from the bogus tree plantation scheme to the crypto trading venture; even some household names that failed to deliver the performance you need for your future.

Like your health care, diet and friendships, share investing can become part of your life. It can be fun and rewarding and when managed properly, keeping your personal limitations and strengths in mind, you might just surprise yourself, in a good way.

Even with my professional experience I needed to tread the path to develop into a sophisticated share investor. My journey has been littered with mistakes that I treat as positive learning experiences, because I always protect my transactions so that if one fails, I am not so heavily invested that it has a bad impact on the total value of my share portfolios. My journey is balanced between learning when to be greedy and learning when to be fearful. To quote the legendary Warren Buffett: 'Be greedy when others are fearful and fearful when others are greedy.'

What I covered in *Shareplicity*

Shareplicity is not your typical self-help book on shares. For starters, my four decades of investing in both a professional and personal capacity have helped me carve out pathways to growing my savings and building wealth for the long term. I know my limitations and readily admit to my weaknesses, but I play to my strengths: the ability to apply time and effort to reading and learning, and seeking out quality expert opinion and companies. In turn, I have translated this into a journey on share investing that at the very least, I think, will challenge the views of existing investors and position new investors to understand the 21st century paradigm of 'this time it's different'.

My aim has been to break down the myths, jargon and complexities of share investing. No matter how much technology, digital disruption and financial analysis is applied, shares basically represent companies. Companies in turn are made up of people and different cultures. Not all companies will be successful; in fact, most will fail eventually.

Shareplicity started by setting the scene for your share investment journey with an unusual analogy – the *Ford v Ferrari* tale. How better to explain to those of you who don't feel any connection to companies than this gripping example of corporate culture played out on the big screen?

Having established that shares are just as much about culture and people as money, you then moved on to understanding the basics with Chapter 2's Sharepedia. It's always good to brush up on the basics; you might come across a term that flips a switch that you hadn't considered in the past. I talked about how compounding is the silver bullet of share investing. The magic of maths allows you to grow your savings over time and that's why it's so important to start as young as you can. Even with a small amount you'll be amazed at how compounding can transform your nest egg into a six-person omelette. Time and patience are your friends.

We touched on the economic mumbo-jumbo of the big and the small economic picture and came away with some important points. Interest rates matter and we're in a lower-growth and lower-for-longer interest rate environment, meaning cash in the bank is letting us down. Of course, we all need to look out for any possible signs of real inflationary pressures, but as I write there are no signs of this on the horizon.

Next you learnt about what makes a good company and there-fore a good share investment. This is one of the themes I'm most passionate about – buying quality companies with sustainable earnings growth. Not only did it serve me well when I advised my clients in the emerging markets, but I have learnt the hard way through my own investing that picking the cyclical shares and bottom fishing the laggards (dogs/losers/underperformers) is very risky. It can deliver big windfalls but it can also leave a big hole in the pocket.

Nothing is risk-free in share investing, but then life isn't a risk-free adventure either, so choose your share investments to meet your risk tolerance and be alert to popping all your eggs in one basket. It can be a game changer for the good, but most likely the bad.

I designed the ASX 30 express as a useful tool for you to under-stand how to look under the bonnet when it comes to analysing shares. The prescribed share ratios like PER and dividend yield go only so far in delivering the answers you want. It's always about the context when you buy shares. In isolation the valuation tools can be misleading. I want you to remember to question why a share is on a low PER: 'is it cheap for a reason?' or 'is it too good to be true?'. Often a high dividend in a low-interest-rate world is a harbinger for bad news around the corner, like a cut in the dividend, a profit downgrade and share price falls. You don't want to own the tensaggers or capital killers.

You learnt how debt in isolation isn't bad; it's all about the cash flow for companies and the ability to match the cash flow with the debt payments. Companies need to grow to make money for shareholders but growth at any cost can lead to disaster.

As you attained a better understanding of cash flow you learnt more about the importance of dividends and how some shares are the dividend champions. No amount of accounting smoke-screens can alter the cash payments. Dividends are the real financial rewards, particularly in down share markets.

I challenged the supremacy of the so-called blue chips and suggested some may become death stars. The share investing world is changing. As we start the third decade of the 21st century there's no better time to reassess your investments. The technical, digital age of disruption is nowhere near finished. There are new themes for investors like the impact of 5G, space travel, cyber security, electric and autonomous cars (my thematic pick for the next decade), renewable and clean energy, and alternative meat products. Don't underestimate climate change risk on shares! These are just a few themes I like and believe will be part of the wealth creators going forward.

You learnt about the market trends of the bulls and the bears, and how emotions of fear and greed play with your investing acumen. Sticking to a plan is important to avoid being dragged into the noise and the momentum trends. For those with an inclination towards charting, I offered my go-to charting point of reference, based on the Dow theory. It's not my preference to work solely with charts and momentum, but over time it may be an avenue you go down. Just remember to define your aims: are you an investor or a trader?

This led you to some of the most important aspects of investing: knowing yourself, understanding the plan so you can develop a pathway that works for you, and building the foundations for saving, investing and creating wealth for whatever you're aiming for.

Not everyone can be an expert and not everyone can invest directly in shares, but don't underestimate what you can achieve. Start small and build your confidence slowly, because no amount of reading and listening is equal to actual experience; good or bad, it all matters. Remember that picking one or two of the winners could be life-changing. We all just need one CSL in our life.

Keep an eye on the costs (management fees, trading fees) as they're problematic when it comes to eroding the performance of your investments. Make the most of the new ETF products that are readily available to Australian investors and which will likely grow in choice. Feel free to flick back and dip into any of the *Shareplicity* chapters at any time.

If you want to read more about analysing shares and review some case studies, you can move on to the appendix. The Boeing example is one of the most interesting and, in time, will be a major case study for business schools. It can also help you understand some of the variables I consider when buying and selling shares.

Thank you for coming with me on the *Shareplicity* journey. It has been a dream of mine to write a book, so I feel so honoured to be able to share my thoughts, processes and pathways to healthy investing. The most important thing I have learnt along the way during my four decades of investing and writing this book is to believe in myself. I want you to believe in yourself as well; share investing isn't rocket science. Anyone can start and hopefully *Shareplicity* has given you the confidence and understanding to succeed in share investing.

Chapter summary

- Lower interest rates for longer means cash in the bank isn't a winner.

- We are in an era of great change and assuming what worked in the past still works could lead to disappointment and poor performance.

- Digital and technical disruption is your friend in terms of lowering the costs of investing and making it easier for everyone to start with as little as $500.

- Continue your journey of investing – experience matters.

- Start as young as you can, but you're never too old to change or learn more.

- Be wary of trading too frequently, looking for a quick profit; investing takes time and the powers of compounding will work magic for your savings.

- When picking shares, remember the numbers only tell half the story; you need to look under the bonnet.

- Quality and culture are very important elements for the wealth maker to understand.

- Pick your investment themes for 21st century investing and remember that great ETFs mean you don't need to invest directly.

- Remember that 'value' and 'cheap' are two different concepts; cheap doesn't always offer value, as cheap can become cheaper.

- Be wary of shares that have very high dividend yields – this is usually a sign that something is amiss.

- Manage your risk and do what works for you.

- Know yourself and match your investing to your strengths and weaknesses.

- Remember to sell the losers and cull the share portfolio or the third party (managed) funds. Relationships don't last forever.

Appendix:
Share investing case studies

These case studies provide insight into some of my thought processes when it comes to buying and selling shares. I haven't always been 100 per cent correct, and I find I can cope better with the bad decisions if I've gone through a mental checklist. Keep in mind that share investing is as much about not losing your capital as it is about making money. You can't kiss all the handsome boys and pretty girls, meaning you can't expect to own every winning share.

So, here are some examples from my years of investing, with a focus on recent cases. Boeing and CSL are great examples of how corporate culture and quality affect shares. The others focus on the lesson I learnt from buying the share.

Boeing: to be patient or not, that is the question

This is a multifaceted example of how difficult it is to assess investment risks when you don't have all the information. Boeing Company is interesting for a number of reasons. Not only is the 100-year-old Boeing a household name but it's also an institution for the airline, aerospace and US defence industries.

Boeing ticks a lot of the boxes highlighting the complexity of share investment: the company is capital intensive and its aircraft production programs are complex, with long lead times to production.

Due to the nature of the business, the company must also interface with many stakeholders, including the aviation authorities, the pilots association, and customers, employees and shareholders. Every time a Boeing plane takes off, its reputation is on the line in terms of safety.

My story regrettably begins with two tragic plane crashes involving the new Boeing 737 Max aircraft within a four-month period, in late 2018 and early 2019, throwing a considerable degree of uncertainty over the share investment.

Up until that point Boeing had been one of the Dow Jones Industrial Index's top performers (as well as a major employer and contributor to US economic activity). It rose from the 2009 share price lows of US$30 to a high above US$440 in late 2018.

Boeing's ongoing earnings success was, and is, geared towards the relatively new 737 Max, which is a revamped version of one of Boeing's most successful aircraft in the company's history.

Two major crashes and the death of 346 passengers and crew led to the grounding of all the 737 Max planes in service in March 2019. At the time of writing 11 months on, the planes are still grounded and production has stopped, with costs escalating to US$10 billion.

In March 2019, when I sold my shares, I was not in receipt of all the information that has since become public. I sold my Boeing shares soon after the second plane crash, at US$384. Since then the share price has fallen to a recent low of US$313, although it previously rallied to US$380. Shareholders have been taken on a roller-coaster ride: first some good news announcements, followed by considerably more bad news with the ongoing delay of lifting the ban on the aircraft until June/July 2020, followed by leaked negative staff emails and concerns over the certification of the 737 Max, and then the cessation of the production of planes. There are 400 planes still to be built. Compensation was offered to airlines that already owned the planes (387 delivered), the CEO (once Chairman) Dennis Mullenburg was sacked and Boeing still needs to raise more debt of an estimated US$10 billion.

Many question marks continue to hang over the future of the 737 Max and whether the aircraft will ever receive certification to fly again.

What has emerged during the Max crisis is how much the Boeing culture changed after the takeover of its rival McDonnell Douglas in 1997. The cost-cutting, profit-oriented model of McDonnell Douglas has seemingly usurped Boeing's historical tradition of placing engineering excellence first. The adaptation of the old 737 Max is a case in point. The engines, although more fuel efficient, are too heavy for the body of the aircraft and placed too far forward, giving potential for the nose of the plane to tilt up in flight and stall. Instead of redesigning the plane (which according to some isn't structurally aerodynamic to fly), Boeing relied on developing a software system to correct the angle of the plane in flight. It was a quicker and more expeditious route to getting a new, more fuel-efficient passenger jet into service, allowing Boeing to compete more effectively against its rival Airbus.

So, basically, Boeing used software to fix a hardware problem. Also, there were question marks over where the sensors had been installed on the Max jets, causing false readings for the pilots. There was also an absence of pilot training for the new software system, meaning when it overrode the pilots (based on false sensor readings) the pilots struggled and ultimately failed to fix the problem.

At the time I sold my Boeing shares, this information was not publicly available and much of it has been slow to come out (for obvious reasons: it's detrimental to the company and the share price). As a shareholder I had to make a decision in the absence of full receipt of all the information I now have. That's what share investing is about.

If I had held the shares, I would have lost a further 15 per cent of my capital and not reinvested the money into another share that would have made money (an opportunity cost).

Investors really should have asked themselves a number of questions after the first or second crash:

- What percentage of Boeing's earnings is estimated to be generated from the production of the new 737 Max and for what period of time?
- If the crashes were correlated, is the problem with the plane or human error?
- If the problems are with the plane, are the issues able to be fixed, what delay will there be and what are the financial consequences for said delays?
- Are the problems of a more substantial nature; are there genuine structural problems that could jeopardise the rollout and future earnings growth source for Boeing?
- What's the reputational risk to the company?

Some of the answers can be found through research and articles published online. The complexity of the issues, however, made it difficult to understand what was really happening in the early days following the incidents. My decision to sell has been vindicated, as no-one knows whether the 737 Max crisis can be solved. Would you fly in one of these aircraft? I know I wouldn't, and Boeing can ill afford another accident.

Sometimes there are just too many risks and unanswered questions. As individuals we don't have to own certain shares, so no matter what the history or tradition, it's sometimes preferable to just get out and revisit the story in the future. Equally, the travails that have beset the company from the 1997 takeover of Boeing's biggest competitor may have created a set of circumstances so deleterious that it will take years for Boeing to recover. You should never underestimate the influence of culture on a company.

CSL: the one I didn't understand

I'm going to put my hand up and say I'm the first to admit I did not understand the CSL story when I started restructuring my share portfolios in 2016. Like many people, I thought the shares seemed too expensive on a high PER multiple. How wrong could I have been? The answer is very! Although the PER multiples have expanded as interest rates have moved down (all PER multiples have increased due to the lower cost of capital interest rates), the CSL share price has been one of the top large market cap performers in Australia (see Chapter 5 for more about CSL).

The lesson here is to be prepared to change your mind. Share prices of good companies can go up for much longer than you expect; sustainable earnings streams and growth in dividends are valuable in the low-interest-rate world we live in. When investigating whether to buy a strong share-price performer like CSL, be careful not to place too much emphasis on how much the shares have risen in the past. Many investors have passed up investing in great companies because they're afraid that the share price has risen too much and must crash. History shows that good companies can increase their earnings, dividends and shares for many decades as long as they keep adapting and investing in future earnings growth.

Annual reporting season is an excellent time for investors to get insight into a company beyond the financial statements and written words. Most companies have annual conference calls that you can join, or you can upload them at your convenience from the investor section of the company's website. The 2019 CSL conference call is a good case in point. Throughout the call, the CEO and CFO cited numerous moat characteristics, as listed below, which continue to help underwrite the robust nature of CSL's business and its ability to maintain profit growth year after year.

In the absence of any experience analysing companies, you need look no further than this list to gain a good overview of the characteristics of a top-performing company. If you find such a company, then buying its shares becomes a matter of price and when the share is offering value – even expensive shares are sold off periodically.

The moat characteristics, or what's also termed 'competitive advantage', are at the heart of what makes a quality company and a dividend champion. Here are some of the main points from the CSL conference call, to offer you insights into the factors that make a great business, company and therefore shareholding:

- a high 25 per cent return on investment capital in 2019

- 8 per cent growth in dividend

- a 21 per cent increase in research and development, constituting 10 per cent spend of total revenue

- capital expenditure that has doubled from 2015 to 2019

- being an ongoing global leader in its markets and strengthening its supply capabilities

- robust supply chains, which is an imperative in the global plasma business

- continued investment in people and improved employee diversity, with women constituting 57 per cent of the CSL workforce

- strong margins

- focus on improving efficiencies

- investment in sourcing of supplies in good locations, notably plasma.

Although there can be some variance between industries, whether it's service based, tech or cyclical, many of the moat characteristics will overlap. The conference calls or any interviews with management are also a great platform to glean a better understanding of the company and the business culture.

Dumb luck with Sarich

In the mid-1980s I bought shares in a company called Sarich that was one of the hot stocks of its era. Known for the development of the 'orbital engine', Sarich's technology was going to supplant the traditional combustion engine. I bought the shares because a stockbroker friend of my mother had high aspirations for the company, like the rest of Australia did. Although my memory of the details is a bit scratchy, I recall that I made a 25 per cent profit in a very short time, before the problems arose.

Sarich shares experienced what I call 'irrational exuberance': lots of hype and hope with no substance (bubble territory). That mood can permeate the share market and shares move based on mere speculation. The technology wasn't proven and yet investors had already calculated how many billions the company could make. Companies with huge growth potential and no strong evidence of achieving said growth can experience massive share price rises. Some investors can make a lot of money along the way and some can lose money if the story doesn't stack up to all the hype and hysteria.

In the Sarich example, the engine was regrettably prone to overheating and would never be commercially viable. Once that became known the shares crashed and many investors lost their money.

I can't emphasise enough how important it is to establish the risks you're taking when investing all your money into one share of a speculative nature. Remember that you only ever hear the good stories; no-one brags about their losses.

The biggest mistake an investor can make is assuming intelligence, good judgement and skill achieved an investment profit. Lady luck is always an integral part of the result. Skill and knowledge can help place an investor in a position where a decision has a greater probability of success, but success should not be assumed and nor is it guaranteed. Sometimes an investment choice has as much to do with timing as skill. Appreciating when good luck is around is as important as acknowledging bad luck happens as well.

For whatever reason I was content to make what seemed at the time a huge profit on my Sarich trade, and I felt disinclined to hope for more. Sarich was a risky share and in such cases it's worthwhile recognising when to take profits. Not all shares should be held forever: sometimes a bird in the hand is worth more than two in the bush.

The accidental tenbagger: a2 Milk

The a2 Milk shares were for many the gift that kept on giving. A few years back, while driving, I heard the ABC interviewing the CEO of a New Zealand dairy company called a2 Milk. The CEO was an excellent marketer. He explained in detail the benefits of the A2 protein and the company's push into the Chinese baby formula market, which had been rocked by the inclusion of melamine in infant formula, milk and other products in around 2008.

The company was and remains a major beneficiary of the clean, green image that New Zealand and Australian dairy produce have in the Chinese market. It had a unique selling point with its a2 protein, which is apparently easier to digest for lactose intolerant consumers.

After some research I decided to buy the shares, which were around the $1.50 level. Nothing happened for ages until the financial results were announced, validating the growth potential of the company, particularly in the Chinese market.

The a2 Milk shares have benefitted from the exponential growth in revenue and earnings over a short space of time. As the shares rose and the story improved I bought more, until I eventually sold out at $12. My decision to sell out at around $12 may seem wrong, considering that the shares first rose to as high as $17 before retracing back to around $14. There was no one reason for my sale. Concerns over the ability of the company to maintain the rate of growth, overlaid with possible Chinese trade issues, competitive pressures from big producers such as Nestle and ethical concerns were some of the reasons.

Over the passage of time, my selling off my a2 Milk shares may not prove to be correct, but I made substantial gains from this investment and am happy to leave the rest to others. Investing in a company like a2 Milk isn't the norm for most of us, particularly if it's in the early stages of an exponential growth trajectory. Picking winners is as much about good process, as it is about skill and luck. I did my research; I also took some profits along the way, before selling the entire holding.

I've heard a lot of stories, particularly from retail investors who are jumping on board to buy stocks, about companies experiencing amazing growth. This is often in sectors that have become fashionable among investors. In the last few years there have been momentum investing fads in a few growth sectors, namely lithium and graphite stocks (for exposure to the electric car market); agricultural/dairy businesses like a2 Milk that are geared to the Chinese domestic consumption market; and medicinal cannabis stocks.

Investors always need to do their homework rather than just looking to anecdotal evidence as a reason to buy a stock. As always, the devil is in the detail and investing trends or fads can attract less optimal companies. A2 Milk was and remains a stand-out company with its unique selling point of an alternative milk protein. Whether it can survive the challenges of competition, historic drought conditions in Australia and other challenges remains to be seen. Sometimes reaping the rewards and moving on is the best outcome for investors.

RCR Tomlinson: that wasn't meant to happen!

As a rule of thumb, if a company issues one or more negative earnings surprises, I usually abandon ship. The company isn't worth the risk. If the share price falls by more than 25 per cent and there's no available news to be found, I'm usually wary but not necessarily alarmed.

It's a shame I didn't listen to my own advice when it came to owning one of Australia's oldest and most reputable engineering contractors, RCR Tomlinson. I was attracted to the narrative (warning!), as they had moved into the solar energy space. I bought shares in the company (albeit not too large a holding), then the share price started falling with no known new information available. It kept falling and every rally turned into a selling event. Remember the Dow theory and the warning signs about when a share makes lower highs and lower lows? Well, this was happening and I was asleep at the wheel.

Even though alarm bells were ringing loudly and I sold some shares, regrettably I did not divest the full shareholding by the time the company was forced into administration (went bankrupt). The speed at which this occurred caught many investors off guard, including some large managed funds.

The company was haemorrhaging significant amounts of cash on unprofitable solar farm contracts, and there were major problems connecting the farms to the grid. RCR Tomlinson basically ran out of money and its debtors, the banks, foreclosed on its loans. I lost the balance of what I had invested in the company.

The good news was that my shareholding was not large enough to make a notable dent in my savings. All the same, no-one likes a loss.

RCR Tomlinson had existed for 150 years. The company was started in 1898 by the Tomlinson brothers and floated in 1951, but an aggressive diversification into fixed price solar contracts was the complete undoing of the business. It collapsed under heavy debts, even after a $100 million equity injection a month before.

I have had similar but not quite so devastating experiences with other contracting firms (think Lendlease and Downer EDI or CIMIC). I have come to the conclusion that being a listed company and a major contractor/developer of large infrastructure is incompatible to shareholders' aspirations. By definition, contractors bid for large engineering projects, which don't always turn out according to plan. It's okay for large companies with a big balance sheet, like Lendlease, but for smaller companies like RCR, losses can quickly cause major cash flow problems.

Afterpay: the one that got away

Afterpay – a fintech, buy-now/pay-later hot stock – is my bête noire, meaning that the share price volatility has tripped me up on a number of occasions. Afterpay is one of the leaders in the buy-now/pay-later segments, with total sales rising 140 per cent in the 2019 results to AUD\$5.2 billion, underpinned by strong growth in the USA and UK.

You can't deny the long-term potential, but the path to shareholder profits has been riddled with road humps along the way, including a few equity capital raisings, some regulatory issues with AUSTRAC, some major shareholder issues (selling down of the founders' stakes), the issuance of employee options to the American staff and the longer-term threat of margin compression from competitive pressures.

Afterpay is more than a modern-day layby company; it's a massive online shopping platform and you can assume it has the capacity for considerable data collation.

The risks associated with such a high-growth new company are often reflected in the volatile share price movements. You should not buy shares that have high volatility, meaning that move up and down by a large percentage often on small volumes, unless you can cope with seeing yourself make and lose money. I do have tolerance for volatility but it's share specific. In this case, owning Afterpay just did not work for me. Despite any upgrades in earnings and buy recommendations I have taken a time-out approach to the shares, as I know all too well that I'll make an error like selling off or buying at the wrong time.

Afterword

At time of going to press, the world's share markets have plunged on fear, uncertainty and panic over the spread of the coronavirus and the potential impacts on the real economies. The fear has been compounded by a crash in the oil price as the major producers Saudi Arabia and Russia embark on a price war.

All share market crashes are scary. This one has come out of the blue from a black swan event, the coronavirus. Share markets do not like uncertainty. Fear and panic beget more fear and panic.

As money around the world flees to safe havens like gold and government bonds, other financial assets such as shares are being sold off heavily and, closer to home, the Australian dollar has come under selling pressure.

It will take time to establish the real economic impacts from the fallout of these events. To date, central banks (including the RBA) have responded with lower interest rates and Australia's federal government has announced its fiscal stimulus package. These measures are designed to take the stress off our financial system and support demand of products and services while there are supply constraints from the virus fallout.

None of these events invalidates the general information explained in *Shareplicity*.

I have seen many crashes in my lifetime and each one is different and no less scary for the investor. However, it remains as true today as 30 years ago, quality shares with strong balance sheets and good cash flow, even in the face of events like these, will survive and will outperform and these periods offer good entry points when the dust settles.

About the author

Danielle Ecuyer pursued a successful career for 15 years in institutional equities stockbroking and wealth management after completing her Commerce degree at the University of New South Wales. She trained and worked as an Australian equities analyst for BZW Australia in Sydney, consolidating her knowledge of fundamental share analysis. In 1990, Danielle moved to London to work in institutional equities sales in global emerging markets and specialised wealth management. Here she was employed in senior positions at some of the world's pre-eminent financial firms in the 1990s and looked after some of the world's largest emerging market investors in a time of great change.

After retiring, Danielle became a full-time investor while raising her son, working for NGOs and pursuing other passions. Now, with over four decades of successful domestic and international experience in share investing in both a professional and personal capacity, Danielle has drawn on her wealth of expertise and wisdom to write *Shareplicity: a simple approach to share investing*.

Her experiences of the investment world as an adviser and client allow her to bring a fresh and independent perspective to share investing. *Shareplicity* aims to educate and inform both new and existing investors, challenge the status quo of Australian 'blue chips', and provide up-to-date data and advice on dividends and 21st century investment themes.

It's one thing to have a couple of good years of investing under your belt, yet another to survive and succeed over the long term. This was Danielle's goal, and she has achieved it. You can too. Whether it's taking the first steps or improving your share investing literacy, *Shareplicity* will help you on the path to realising your financial goals and dreams.

Glossary of financial terms

All Ordinaries. A market capitalisation-weighted index of all stocks listed on the *ASX* which satisfy various liquidity and free-float requirements. Once the Australian stock market benchmark, it has since been replaced in that role by the *S&P/ASX 200* index.

Alpha. The risk associated with, or stock price movement attributable to, factors specific to an individual stock and not to the market as a whole (beta).

Assets under management (AUM). The total market value of assets held in a fund, such as a *real estate investment trust*.

ATO. Acronym for the Australian Taxation Office.

Australian Securities Exchange (ASX) (also known as the Australian stock market). Australia's electronic trading exchange through which Australian shares and other listed financial instruments are bought and sold. The exchange is a listed company called ASX Ltd with the stock code ASX.

Capital expenditure (capex). Money invested by a company in plant and equipment which is carried as assets on the balance sheet.

Capital gains tax (CGT). Tax investors pay on profits when they sell their shareholdings.

Capital gains tax (CGT) discount. Individual investors may be eligible for a 50% CGT discount on profits from an investment held for longer than 12 months.

Capitalisation. See *market capitalisation*.

CHESS (Clearing House Electronic Subregister System). The *ASX*'s computer system used to register shareholdings and manage share transactions.

Compound annual growth rate (CAGR). The annual growth rate of an investment over time, including reinvesting the profits, usually expressed as a percentage.

Compounding. When the interest on the principal or the dividend income on shares is reinvested in the original amount to increase the total returns over time.

Corporate bonds. Instead of shares, companies can issue corporate bonds (to raise money) as a debt instrument that has defined characteristics depending the issue (duration and interest paid). Corporate bonds rate higher than shares if a company is wound up.

Cum dividend. Denoting shares that are eligible for an upcoming dividend. If a share is cum dividend, the share price seems somewhat inflated as it reflects its value plus the dividend that the shareholder is about to receive.

Dividend (also known as distribution). This is the money shareholders 'earn' from holding a share. Dividends are usually paid twice a year from the profits made by the company they have invested in.

Dividend per share (DPS). A listed company's dividends paid over a period divided by the total shares held by investors ('shares outstanding'); the amount paid to each shareholder out of the earnings per share.

Dividend reinvestment plan (DRP). While dividends are typically paid in cash, from time to time companies may offer shareholders the choice of taking their dividend in new shares to the equivalent value. DRPs incrementally increase capital.

Dividend yield. In simple terms, this is the amount shareholders earn from their investment by way of a *dividend* or distribution. It's calculated as the annual *dividend per share* divided by the share price, expressed as a percentage per annum. Historical *yield* is last year's dividend over today's share price, forward yield is forecast dividend over today's share price, and the yield achieved by a shareholder is the dividend divided by the price of entry into the stock.

Earnings before interest and tax (EBIT). A company's profits in a defined period before deducting interest charges and tax.

Earnings before interest, tax, depreciation and amortisation (EBITDA). A company's profits in a defined period before deducting interest charges, tax, depreciation and amortisation.

Earnings per share (EPS). A listed company's net profit for a period divided by the number of shares outstanding (held by investors) on the stock exchange.

Exchange traded fund (ETF). A low-cost passive listed fund that represents a share index, a sector, currencies or bonds.

Ex-dividend date. The day after the *record date* for dividends. Denoting shares that don't have the value of a dividend included in their price. Shares often trade lower on the ex-dividend date to reflect the payment of the dividend that's just been made.

Financial year (FY). The 12-month period over which a company accounts for its business. Typically in Australia this is July–June but some companies run on different cycles.

Float. See *initial public offering*.

Franking. An Australian shareholder only pays tax on a company's profit once. If that company has paid all its tax in Australia, then the dividend paid to a shareholder isn't taxed again but 'fully franked'. Levels of franking less than 100 per cent imply that a company has earned a proportion of its profit offshore or has received tax rebates (for example, for exploration expenses) and so not paid 'full' tax. Foreign investors are not eligible for franking.

Franking credits. The rebate shareholders can claim if they have received fully franked dividends (see also *franking*).

Funds under management (FUM). The total market value of funds being managed by a fund manager.

Government bonds. Governments issue bonds (debt instruments) to raise money. The terms will differ depending upon the government and the time frame the bonds are issued for.

Gross domestic product (GDP). The total value of goods and services produced by a nation over one year. GDP measures the total output from all resources located in the country, wherever the owners of the resources live.

Inflation. The term for the rise in prices of goods and services and of wages over time.

Initial public offering (IPO). When a company lists its shares for the first time on the share market (also referred to as a 'float' or 'listing').

Institutional investors. Funds, superannuation funds, companies and banks that invest at scale in the stock market.

Listed investment company (LIC). Similar to a *LIT*, except it has shares (not units) listed on the stock exchange and the company status allows it to manage how it pays out the *dividends* and *franking credits*. That is, unlike for a LIT, all the dividend payments don't have to be distributed each year, they can be carried over and the income streams smoothed over time. The shares can trade at a discount or premium to the net tangible assets/net asset value, depending on shareholder demand.

Listed investment trust (LIT). A closed fund that has a fixed number of units available to buy on the stock exchange. The fund invests in shares and the shareholder receives the dividend income. Often LITs trade at a discount to the *net asset value*, meaning the share price doesn't fully reflect the value of the trust.

Managed funds (mFunds). Financial instruments that give access to funds not listed on the ASX.

Market capitalisation or 'market cap' (sometimes simply called 'capitalisation'). The value of a stock implied by the current share price multiplied by the number of ordinary shares on issue.

Net asset value (NAV). The value of a company's assets divided by the number of shares on issue.

Net interest cover. This is a ratio calculated by dividing EBIT (earnings before interest and tax) by interest expense less interest income.

Net interest margin (NIM). In simple terms, the difference between the net rate at which a bank borrows money and the net rate at which the bank lends money.

Net profit after tax (NPAT). An accounting term that measures for a company how much profit is left after the costs of operating the business have been deducted.

Net tangible assets (NTA). Today's value of a company's tangible assets (such as buildings), not intangible assets (such as goodwill). An important measure for property trusts.

Payout ratio. A listed company's total dividends divided by its net profit, expressed as a percentage.

Price to earnings ratio (PER) (also referred to as P/E ratio). The current stock price of a company divided by past earnings (historical PER) or forecast earnings (forward PER) expressed as a multiple (for example, 10x). PERs are effectively a measure of market sentiment, as a higher PER implies a greater demand for a stock and a lower PER lesser demand, all else (earnings) being equal.

Quantitative easing (QE). An alternative monetary policy tool for central banks to cutting cash rates. The central bank buys bonds issued by the government (or corporates), which keeps rates low.

Real estate investment trust (REIT). A property fund listed on the stock exchange. Australian REITs are known as AREITs.

Record date. The last day that a shareholder is eligible for a *dividend*.

Reporting season. The period during which companies report their earnings – usually twice yearly in Australia.

Retail investors (also called 'mum and dad investors'). These are individual investors rather than institutional investors (funds, companies and banks).

Return on equity. The percentage return annually on shareholder's funds. Net income divided by shareholders' equity.

Rights issue. When a company offers new shares to shareholders to raise money.

S&P/ASX 200. The Standard & Poor's/ASX index of the 200 largest stocks on the ASX weighted by *market capitalisation*. When introduced in 2000 it replaced the *All Ordinaries* as Australia's stock market benchmark. Other major indices include the S&P/ASX 20, 100 and 300.

Secular market. A market that's being driven by factors that underpin long-term growth in the market, unaffected by short-term trends.

Self managed account (SMA). An account offered to investors via a platform like Praemium, in which the investor holds the shares or securities directly but a third party decides which shares to hold. Fees apply.

Share (also called stock or equity). A shareholder's part-ownership of a listed company represented by a price on the share market.

Share portfolio. A group of shares an individual invests in over time, designed to meet their investment needs.

Share purchase plan (SPP). Typically accompanying an institutional placement, an SPP allows *retail investors* to participate in a company's capital raising on a book-build basis, meaning the balance of supply and demand determines the final purchase price.

Share split. When a company divides its shares into more shares and gives shareholders extra shares, but the total value of each shareholding remains the same. As a result, each shareholder owns more shares, but each individual share is worth less.

Shareholders' equity. This is the money you and others own in a company when you buy its listed shares.

Volatility. Put simply, this is how much a share price or market goes up and down. In a volatile market, prices are rising then falling frequently over a short period of time.

Yield. *See dividend yield.*

YOY. Acronym used in the financial markets meaning 'year on year'.

Index